Rashomon / Yam Gruel

by Ryunosuke Akutagawa

Level 5

Translated by Michael Brase

IBC パブリッシング

はじめに

ラダーシリーズは、「はしご（ladder）」を使って一歩一歩上を目指すように、学習者の実力に合わせ、無理なくステップアップできるよう開発された英文リーダーのシリーズです。

リーディング力をつけるためには、繰り返したくさん読むこと、いわゆる「多読」がもっとも効果的な学習法であると言われています。多読では、「1. 速く 2. 訳さず英語のまま 3. なるべく辞書を使わず」に読むことが大切です。スピードを計るなど、速く読むよう心がけましょう（たとえば TOEIC® テストの音声スピードはおよそ1分間に150語です）。そして1語ずつ訳すのではなく、英語を英語のまま理解するくせをつけるようにします。こうして読み続けるうちに語感がついてきて、だんだんと英語が理解できるようになるのです。まずは、ラダーシリーズの中からあなたのレベルに合った本を選び、少しずつ英文に慣れ親しんでください。たくさんの本を手にとるうちに、英文書がすらすら読めるようになってくるはずです。

《本シリーズの特徴》

- 中学校レベルから中級者レベルまで５段階に分かれています。自分に合ったレベルからスタートしてください。
- クラシックから現代文学、ノンフィクション、ビジネスと幅広いジャンルを扱っています。あなたの興味に合わせてタイトルを選べます。
- 巻末のワードリストで、いつでもどこでも単語の意味を確認できます。レベル１、２では、文中の全ての単語が、レベル３以上は中学校レベル外の単語が掲載されています。
- カバーにヘッドホーンマークのついているタイトルは、オーディオ・サポートがあります。ウェブから購入／ダウンロードし、リスニング教材としても併用できます。

《使用語彙について》

レベル１：中学校で学習する単語約 1000 語

レベル２：レベル１の単語＋使用頻度の高い単語約 300 語

レベル３：レベル１の単語＋使用頻度の高い単語約 600 語

レベル４：レベル１の単語＋使用頻度の高い単語約 1000 語

レベル５：語彙制限なし

Contents

Rashomon

Rashomon 「羅生門」

【あらすじ】

ある日の夕暮れどき、一人の下人が荒れ果てた羅生門の下で雨宿りをしていた。時は平安時代、都はこの2、3年の天災や火事、飢饉で著しく衰微していた。下人は数日前に職を失い、もはや盗人になるしかないと思いつめていたが、その決心ができずにいた。門の上の楼閣で夜を明かそうと幅の広い梯子を上がった下人は、そこにうち棄てられた多くの身寄りのない遺体の間で、何者かの気配を感じた。

【登場人物】

servant 下人　職を失い生活に困っている男。右のほほに大きなニキビがある

old woman 老婆　背の低い、やせた、猿のような老女

【羅城門（羅生門）について】

「羅城門」とは、都城を取り囲む城壁である「羅城(らじょう)」に設けられた門のことで、中世頃からは「羅生門」とも表記されるようになりました。平安京の羅城門は、朱雀大路の南端（北端は朱雀門）にあり、京の都への正門として用いられていました。816年（弘仁7年）8月16日夜に大風で倒壊し、一度は再建されますが、平安中後期に入ると社会の乱れとともに治安が悪化、この物語が書かれた頃には、門はすでに荒廃しており、上層は死体置き場として用いられていました。その後980年（天元3年）7月9日の暴風雨で再度損傷してから以後は再建計画が上がるも、実際に再建されることはありませんでした。

■日本語原文

https://www.aozora.gr.jp/cards/000879/card127.html（青空文庫）
https://ja.wikisource.org/wiki/羅生門（ウィキソース）

It happened one day as the sun was setting. A low-ranking servant was waiting beneath Rashomon gate for the rain to let up.

There was no one else under the huge gate. The only other living creature there was a cricket sitting on one of the large columns whose red lacquer had begun to flake. Since Rashomon stood on Suzaku Avenue leading to the Imperial Palace, one would ordinarily expect to find two or three men or women wearing courtly headgear waiting for a lull in the rain, but in fact this man was the only person there.

The reason for this was that, in the last two or three years, Kyoto had suffered from a series of earthquakes, twisters, fires and famine, and the city had deteriorated dreadfully.

According to ancient documents, Buddhist statues and wooden religious fittings were broken up, stacked in piles, and sold for firewood on the roadside, even though some of them still retained their original silver and gold leaf and their lacquer coating. With the city itself in such a terrible state, no one was willing to take responsibility for repairing Rashomon. Taking advantage of the dilapidated condition of the gate, foxes and badgers began to live there. Thieves made it their home. Bodies of the dead without close kin were customarily abandoned there. This being the case, with the descent of the sun, no one lingered long near Rashomon if they could possibly help it.

On the other hand, the gate attracted large flocks of crows from somewhere nearby. In the daytime, a number of them could be heard cawing as they flew in circles around the decorative tile-ends high on the roof. Particularly at sunset, when the sky was still aglow, their forms stood out quite clearly, like black seeds that had been sown in the sky. It hardly needs saying that the crows came to feast on the corpses to be found on the gate's second floor. Tonight, however, perhaps because of the lateness of the hour, there was not a single crow to be seen. On the crumbling stone steps leading up to the gate, grass grew freely out of the cracks, and here and there were patches of white crow droppings. The servant was sitting on the topmost of the seven steps wearing a washed-out dark-blue kimono. Fingering a large pimple on his right cheek, he was gazing vacantly at the falling rain.

I said that the servant was "waiting for a lull in the rain," but in fact, even if the rain did stop, he had nothing particular in mind to do. Ordinarily, he would return to his place of employment, but the truth of the matter was that four days ago he had been given his walking papers. As mentioned above, Kyoto at this time was going through a period of extraordinary decline. The dismissal of a servant was just one small ripple effect of this decline. That is why, rather than saying that the servant was waiting for the rain to let up, it would be more appropriate to say that he was trapped by the rain without anywhere to go—that is, he was at a loss for what to do. Moreover, the gloomy weather hanging over the city this day stimulated the sentimentalism of this Heian servant. The rain began to fall past the Hour of the Monkey [4:00 PM], and it showed no signs of ceasing. Tomorrow, in any case, he had to find a way of surviving. That is, he was thinking of how to extricate himself from a basically inextricable situation, one thought rambling after another, listening without listening for some time now to the rain falling on Suzaku Avenue.

The rain enveloped Rashomon, pouring down with a rushing sound that came from afar. The advancing dusk gradually darkened the sky until, looking up, the slanting tiles of the roof seemed to be supporting the weight of the lowering clouds.

To make the best of a hopeless situation, he couldn't afford to be too picky about the means he employed. If he was too scrupulous, he might starve to death beside a mud wall or by the side of a road. From there he would be brought to Rashomon's second floor and tossed inside like a miserable dog. On the other hand, if he wasn't particular about the means he employed—and in his mind he had been over this ground many times before reaching this point—the "if" in "if he wasn't particular" would remain forever an "if." Thus, while affirming that he couldn't be picky about the means he employed, he didn't have the courage to positively conclude that "he should become a thief."

The man sneezed loudly and rose wearily to his feet. Kyoto grew chilly in the evening, and it was cold enough now to cause one to wish for a brazier. The wind and settling dusk moved relentlessly through the columns of the gate. The cricket that had been resting on a pillar was no longer there.

The man tucked his head down against the cold and raised the shoulders of his dark-blue kimono and its thin yellow undergarments, surveying the surroundings of the gate. If there was someplace away from the wind and rain, someplace away from the eyes of others, someplace where he could sleep peacefully, that is where he would spend the night. Fortunately, it was then that he noticed a wide, red-lacquered ladder leading up to the second floor of the gate. Up there, if anyone should be present, it would only be the bodies of the dead. The man placed one of his straw-sandaled feet on the first rung of the ladder, being careful that his simple wooden-hilted sword did not slip out of its sheath.

Several minutes passed. The figure of the servant could be seen midway up the ladder, crouched over like a cat and holding his breath, eyeing the interior of the second floor. A ray of light from above shone faintly on his right cheek. It was this cheek, covered by a short beard, that had a red pimple filled with pus. From the beginning the servant had perhaps too easily assumed that the second story would be occupied only by the dead. Going up two or three rungs of the ladder, however, he realized that someone had lit a light and was moving it this way and that. This dull, yellowish, trembling light was reflected off the cobwebs that covered the ceiling of the second floor from corner to corner, and the servant immediately recognized the light for what it was. On a rainy night like this, anyone who would light a lantern on the second floor of

Rashomon must be an extraordinary person indeed.

Moving as silently as a gecko, the servant finally made his way to the last rung of the steep ladder. There he made his body as small as possible, and sticking his head out as far as he could, he peered cautiously inside the second floor.

What he saw, as predicted by rumor, was a good many casually abandoned corpses. However, the space revealed by the light was smaller than expected, making it impossible to determine the number of bodies. It was possible, however, though only faintly, to see that some the bodies were fully clothed while others were not. They seemed to be a mixture of men and women. It was hard to believe that all these bodies had once been living things, for they now looked like dolls made of clay—some with their mouths open, some with their arms outstretched, all rolling on the floor. Moreover, the higher areas of the body—the chest and shoulders—shown faintly with reflected light; the lower areas sank even further into shadow, creating a feeling of eternal silence.

The servant suddenly covered his nose against the putrid smell of the decomposing bodies. In the next moment, however, his hand gave up that task. Another overwhelming emotion deprived him of any sense of smell.

It was then that his eyes first saw a human figure squatting among the bodies. It was an old woman wearing a dark-red kimono. She was short, emaciated, white-haired, and had a monkey-like look about her. Holding a pine torch in her right hand, she was examining the head of one of the corpses. Judging from the length of the corpse's hair, it was most likely a woman.

Moved six parts by fear and four parts by curiosity, the servant almost forgot to breathe. His feelings might be expressed in the words of an ancient writer who said, "The hair on my head and body stood on end." Then the old woman inserted her torch into a crack between the floorboards and placed both hands on the head of the body she had been examining; next, just as a mother monkey might pick lice off a child, the old woman began pulling out the corpse's long hair one at a time. It seemed to come out easily, not resisting the movement of her hand.

As one long hair was removed and then another, the servant felt his feelings of fear gradually diminish. At the same time he felt the gradual growth of a violent hatred for the old woman.—No, it would be misleading to say it was a hatred of the old woman; it was rather a feeling of hate for all evil, which was growing more intense minute by minute. At this point, if someone had brought up the issue that the servant had been contemplating beneath the gate—whether it was better to die of starvation or to become a thief—the servant would have chosen starvation without hesitation or regret. Just like the pine torch that the old woman had stuck between the floorboards, the servant's hatred of evil was growing ever more intense.

Of course, the servant didn't know why the old woman was pulling out the hair of the dead. So, logically, he didn't know whether it should be considered good or evil. But on a rainy night like this, on the second story of the Rashomon gate, the act of removing the hair of the dead seemed an unforgivable act in itself. Naturally, he had entirely forgotten the fact that he himself, a short time ago, had considered becoming a thief.

It was at this point that the servant, with

all the strength his legs possessed, abruptly leaped up from the ladder into the room. With his hand on his sword he strode quickly up to the old woman. Needless to say, she was astounded.

With one look at the servant the old woman leaped into the air as if shot out of a cannon.

"Hey, old hag! What are you up to?"

The servant shouted out and barred her way as she scrambled in a panic through the bodies of the dead. Undaunted, she attempted to push him aside. The servant blocked her way and pushed her back. For a while the two struggled wordlessly among the corpses. The outcome, of course, was clear from the start. Finally the servant grabbed her arm and twisted her body down. Her arm resembled a chicken's leg, nothing but skin and bone.

"What were you doing just now? Out with it! If you don't tell me, this is what you'll get."

So saying, he unsheathed his sword and thrust its blade in front of her face. But still she refused to say a word. She just stood there stubbornly speechless — her hands trembling, her breathing heavy, her eyes seeming ready to pop out of her head. It was then, seeing her thus, that he realized that her entire being was subject to his will. And it was this realization that cooled the fervent fire in his heart against evil without his knowing it. What remained was the tranquil pride and satisfaction that comes when a certain job is accomplished satisfactorily. Looking down on the old woman, the servant said:

"I am not from the Police and Judicial Office or the like. I just happened to be passing by the gate just now. So I am not going to bind you with a rope and take you into custody or anything. All you have to do is tell me what you are doing up here at this time of night."

When the servant had finished, the wide-eyed old woman looked fixedly into his face with even wider eyes. Behind their red eyelids, her eyes were as sharp as those of a predatory bird. Then, as if chewing something, she moved her lips, which the wrinkles on her face had joined to her nose. In her scrawny throat her spiky Adam's apple could be seen moving. From that same throat, like the cawing of a crow, her voice reached his ears, gasping breathlessly.

"By plucking this hair...pulling out this hair...a wig is what I was going to make."

The servant was disappointed to find the old woman's answer so commonplace. Along with this disappointment, he simultaneously felt his prior hatred of evil doings change into an icy contempt for the old woman. Perhaps this change was transmitted to her, for still holding in one hand the long hair she had taken from the corpse, she mumbled the following words in a voice that resembled the croaking of a toad.

"Truly, taking the hair of the dead may be a horrible thing. But the dead you see here all deserved that much. The woman whose hair I was plucking just now would cut up snake meat, dry it, and sell it as fish to the Imperial Palace Guards. Had she not fallen sick and died, she would probably still be doing it. Over and above that, her dried fish was considered tasty, and so the Guards bought it as the main dish of their meal. As for me I don't think what she did was wrong. Otherwise, she would have starved to death, so it was done out of necessity. That's why I can't think what I am doing is wrong. I do it to keep from starving, because it can't be helped. Even this woman, knowing how hard life can be, would understand what I am doing."

This is the gist of what the old woman said.

Returning his sword to its sheath and holding its hilt with his left hand, the servant listened coldly to her story. At the same time he was fingering the large, red, pus-filled pimple on his cheek with his right hand. However, as he listened to her, his heart began to fill with a certain kind of courage. It was the courage that he had lacked when down in front of the gate. It was a courage that went in the opposite direction from the courage that he had displayed when he ascended to the second story and confronted the old woman. He was no longer bothered by the question if he starved to death or became a thief. Judging from his feelings, the issue of starvation had been pushed so far outside his conscious mind that it was hardly worth consideration.

"So that's the way it is," the servant said in a mocking voice as if to confirm what the old woman had said. Then he took a stride forward, removed his right hand from the pimple and grabbed her by the scruff of the neck, spitting out the words, "Don't hold this against me. It is either this or starving to death."

He quickly stripped her of her kimono, and when the old woman clung to his legs, he kicked her onto the pile of bodies. The entrance to the ladder was only a matter of five steps. With her dark-red kimono under his arm, he instantly disappeared down the steep ladder and into the depths of the night.

For a while the old woman remained motionless among the bodies as if dead herself. Then she raised up her naked body, muttering and groaning to herself. She crawled to the entrance of the ladder well, using the light of the torch as a guide. From there she peered down toward the front of the gate, her short hair standing on end. Outside there was nothing to be seen but the pitch dark of night.

What happened to the servant after that? No one knows.

Yam Gruel

Yam Gruel 「芋粥」

【あらすじ】

平安時代、摂政藤原基経に仕える侍の中に「五位」と呼ばれる小役人がいた。五位は、赤鼻で風采が上がらない40歳過ぎの小男で、臆病で意気地がなく、同僚に馬鹿にされたり子供たちに罵られても笑ってごまかして過ごしていた。そんな五位には、宴会の残り物でわずかにもらえるだけの芋粥を、一度飽きるほど食べてみたいというひそかな望みがあった。ある日それを聞いた藤原利仁が「望みを叶えてやろう」と申し出た。

【主な登場人物】

Fifth Ranker 五位　40代の意気地のない小男の侍
Fujiwara no Mototsune 藤原基経　五位が仕えている摂政
a certain samurai without rank 無位の侍　五位をひそかに敬っている
Fujiwara no Tosihito 藤原利仁　五位に芋粥をごちそうする
Fujiwara no Arihito 藤原有仁　利仁の舅

【飽きるほど食べたい「芋粥」とは？】

本作の主人公である五位が一度は飽きるほど食べてみたいと願っていた芋粥。「芋の入った粥」をイメージしてしまいますが全く別のものです。本文中でも記述がありますが、平安時代に宮中の宴会などで最後の方に登場する由緒あるデザートで、ヤマノイモ（自然薯）を薄く切って、甘葛（あまづら）というツタの樹液（みせん）で粥状になるまで煮た甘いスイーツです。さらりとした甘みの汁と、芋のシャクっとした歯触りで、上品な汁粉のように食べられるそうです。

■日本語原文
https://www.aozora.gr.jp/cards/000879/card55.html（青空文庫）
https://ja.wikisource.org/wiki/芋粥（ウィキソース）

This story takes place sometime around the end of the Gankyo era (877–885) or the beginning of the Ninna era (885–889). But the era name does not play an important part in the story; the reader only needs to know that it takes place against the background of the long-ago Heian period.

At the time, among the samurai serving the regent Fujiwara no Mototsune was a certain samurai of the fifth rank.

Here, rather than saying "a certain samurai," I would prefer to explicitly give the person's name, but unfortunately his name has not come down to us in the old documents. It is probably a case of this person being so undistinguished that his name was not considered worth mentioning. From the beginning, the authors of the old documents were apparently not very interested in commonplace people or events. In this respect, they were quite different from modern Japanese Naturalist writers; the writers of the Heian period were not interested in trivial details.

In any case, a certain Fifth Ranker was among the samurai who served Regent Fujiwara no Mototsune. He is the protagonist of this story.

The Fifth Ranker was not an impressive-looking man. First, he was short. Next, he had a red nose, and then his eyes slanted downward. Perhaps not surprisingly, his mustache was sparse, making his jaw look narrower than it was. His lips—well, perhaps it is useless here to recite an endless list of his shortcomings. It is enough to say that the Fifth Ranker presented an extraordinarily unimpressive appearance.

No one knew how or when he first come into the employ of the regent. However, everyone was fully aware that a certain person had been tirelessly carrying out the same daily tasks for quite some time, wearing the same faded informal *suikan* clothing and donning the same droopy headgear. Looking at him now, no one could imagine that he had once been young. (The Fifth Ranker had passed the age of 40.) On the other hand, you couldn't help but feel that his chilly-looking red nose and his token mustache had been blown by the wind coming down Suzaku Avenue since the time he was born. From the regent on down to the children who herded the oxen, no one doubted this fact, albeit unconsciously.

Given his pathetic appearance, there is little need to describe how he was regarded by those around him. The other members of the Samurai Guardhouse paid as much attention to him as they would to a fly. Both those with rank and those without, all the nearly twenty samurai in the Guardhouse were unbelievably indifferent to his comings and goings, almost to the point of downright coldness. When the Fifth Ranker asked them to do something, they didn't even stop chatting among themselves. To them, just as the existence of the air was invisible, so the existence of the Fifth Ranker failed to register on their minds. And if this was the case with the lower rankers, it was only natural that higher officials should ignore him from the very beginning. When dealing with the Fifth Ranker, such people would mostly hide a meaningless and childish maliciousness behind cold looks, communicating with him through gestures. There is a reason that human beings possess language, which is why these officials found that gestures were sometimes insufficient. However, these higher officials thought this was due to the Fifth Ranker's lack of understanding. When this happened, these officials would look him over from top to bottom, from droopy hat to worn straw sandals, then give a snort of laughter and abruptly turn their backs on him. Even so, the Fifth Ranker never got angry. He never took wrong doing as wrong. In fact, he didn't have a backbone. He was a coward.

As if this were not enough, his fellow samurai went out of their way to make him the butt of their jokes. The older among them would recall old quips about his less than elegant appearance, and the younger would practice improvising witty stories based on older witticisms. They would also, in front of the man himself, join in appraising the quality of his nose, his mustache, his hat, his clothing—never seeming to tire of it. But that was not all. Now and then they would also take up the story of the woman with a protruding lower lip who the Fifth Ranker had divorced five or six years ago and the sake-loving Buddhist monk with whom the woman had had an affair. Sometimes they would go beyond this and play some wicked practical jokes on him, though I can't list them all individually here. Perhaps you can imagine the rest if I say that once, after drinking all the sake in his bamboo flask, they had refill the flask with urine.

However, the Fifth Ranker was entirely immune to all this ridicule. Or at least he seemed immune to the eyes of an outsider. No matter what was said of him, the expression on his face remained unchanged. Silently stroking his sparse mustache, he would continue doing whatever he was doing, regardless of the bullying and abuse. But when his fellow samurai's practical jokes went too far, such as when they stuck pieces of paper on his topknot or tied straw sandals to the sheath of his sword, his face would assume an expression halfway between laughing and crying, and he would say, "Oh, that's not nice." Anyone hearing that voice or seeing that face couldn't help being moved. (The effects of this bullying were not confined to the bullying of the Fifth Ranker alone. In fact, many other people unknown to the Fifth Ranker's bullies also became their victims.) These victims adopted the facial expression and tone of voice of the bullied Fifth Ranker as their identifying symbol and as a sign of reproach.—This feeling of reproach, while indistinct, flooded their hearts for a moment. But those who could maintain such a feeling for long were extremely rare. Among them was a certain samurai without rank. He was a young man from Tanba whose soft mustache had barely taken form beneath his nose. At the beginning, of course, he ridiculed the Fifth Ranker like everyone else for no particular reason. But then one day, he happened to hear the Fifth Ranker say, "Oh, that's not nice," and after that he couldn't get those words out of his mind. He came to see the Fifth Ranker as an entirely different person. He could see the "human being" in the Fifth Ranker's impoverished appearance, his pale complexion, his foolish face, and his whimpering when confronted with the world's abuse. Whenever this samurai of no rank thought of the Fifth Ranker, everything in the world suddenly appeared in its basic meanness. At the same time, he couldn't help but feel that the Fifth Ranker's poor red nose and his other pathetic features brought to his heart a strange sense of comfort...

However, this feeling was confined to this one person. Aside from this exceptional case, the Fifth Ranker had to live, as before, the pathetic life of a stray dog amid the contempt of those around him. For one thing, he hardly had a kimono worthy of the name in his possession. He had a bluish-gray formal *suikan* and ballooning-trousers called *sashinuki* of the same color, one pair each. Now both had become so faded that they could no longer be called indigo or dark blue. The shoulders of the *suikan* had fallen a bit, and the color of the braided cord and sash fastener had become somewhat degraded, and there was a good deal of wear around the hem of the *sashinuki*. Seeing the scrawny legs of the Fifth Ranker protruding from the pantless *sashinuki*, even those who were not among his regular bullies couldn't help but feel somewhat wretched themselves, as if they were witnessing the progress of a emaciated ox pulling a carriage of an emaciated nobleman. As for the sword he carried, it was an extremely sorry piece of work, with the gold on the hilt poorly done, and the black lacquer on the sheathe beginning to flake. This was the figure that the red-nosed Fifth Ranker presented, shuffling negligently along in worn straw sandals. In addition to being naturally stooped, he was hunched over further against the cold. Mincing along in tiny footsteps, he continually looked to left and right, as if hungrily searching for something. He presented such a sight that it was not surprising that even passing peddlers made fun of him. In fact, one day the following incident occurred.

One day the Fifth Ranker was going through Sanjobomon gate toward Shinsen'en garden when he saw six or seven children gathered at the roadside doing something. Thinking they might be spinning tops, he looked at what they were engaged in from behind and saw that they had put a rope around the neck of a shaggy stray dog and were beating it with a stick. Until now, whenever the timorous Fifth Ranker encountered something that drew his sympathy, he had never once expressed it. In this case, however, since the other party consisted of children, he managed to work up a bit of courage. Smiling as best he could, he tapped the boy who was apparently the oldest on the shoulder and said,

"That's about enough, I think. Even a dog feels pain." The boy turned toward the Fifth Ranker, his eyes lifted up as if seeing something surprising. He goggled the Fifth Ranker from head to toe as he might view something of a lower order. It was the same expression that the *betto* of the Guardhouse used when he was having trouble communicating with the Fifth Ranker. "It's none of your business," the boy said. Taking a step back, he haughtily added, "What do you want, Red Nose?" To the Fifth Ranker, these words were like a slap in the face. But it wasn't that he was vexed by having a personal flaw pointed out; it was rather that he had spoken up when there was no need to do so and humiliated himself in the process. He tried to hide this awkwardness behind a forced smile, and without saying anything further continued walking toward Shinsen'en. Behind him, the children stood in a line sticking out their tongues in derision. Naturally, the Fifth Ranker knew nothing of this. Even if he did know, what meaning would it have for a weak-kneed person like him...

Well, then, is it fair to say that the protagonist of this story was born into the world simply to be bullied, without any particular desires in life? No, that is not the case. For the last five or six years he had been particularly obsessed by yam gruel. Yam gruel is a porridge with pieces of cut yam boiled in the juice of a sweetener called *amazura*. At the time it was considered the greatest of delicacies and deemed fit for the table of an emperor. People like our Fifth Ranker could expect to experience its delights only once year at a special unofficial banquet. Even then, the amount he could partake of was just enough to whet his appetite. That's why, for some time now, it had been his sole desire to eat as much yam gruel as he could hold. He had not, of course, disclosed this desire to anyone. No, not even he himself was fully conscious of the fact that this desire ran through his life. Without exaggeration, you could say that this is what gave his life meaning.—There are times when a person will sacrifice everything for a desire that he is unsure of gaining. Those who laugh at such foolishness are nothing but bystanders in the drama of life.

However, the Fifth Ranker's dream of "gorging himself on yam gruel" came to be realized with unexpected ease. It is the purpose of this story to tell how that came about.

* * *

On January 2 of a certain year a so-called "special unofficial banquet" took place at the mansion of the regent Fujiwara no Mototsune. (This special unofficial banquet was held at the residence of an advisor/regent of the emperor on the same day as the Imperial Feast attended by the Crown Prince and Empress and by invited nobility of minister rank and below; otherwise it was in no way different from an Imperial Feast.) The Fifth Ranker, along with other samurai, partook of the food left over from the banquet. The custom of throwing leftovers into the garden to be picked up and eaten by lesser beings had not yet been established. Rather the samurai of the house customarily gathered in a hall and feasted on the remains of the banquet there. Of course, even though this banquet can be said to be equivalent to an Imperial Feast, we are talking about the distant past when the number of dishes was large but individually nothing to boast about. Among the dishes was *futo* rice cake, steamed abalone, dried bird meat, Uji whitebait, Omi *funa*, dried slices of sea bream, salmon eggs, grilled octopus, large shrimp, large tangerines, small tangerines, citrus fruit, persimmons dried on skewers, and other such things. Among them was to be found yam gruel. Every year the Fifth Ranker looked forward to the yam gruel. However, since the gathering consisted of a large number of people, the amount of gruel left to him was always rather meager. This year it was particularly small. Possibly for that reason, the gruel tasted much better than it usually did. After finishing the yam he looked steadily at the empty bowl. And wiping the drops that clung to his mustache with the palm of his hand, he said to no one in particular, "I wonder if there will ever be a time when I tire of eating yam gruel."

"The Fifth Ranker never tires of yam gruel, I hear," someone mockingly shouted out when the Fifth Ranker had hardly finished speaking.

It was a husky, easygoing laugh, apparently that of a military man. Much in the manner of the timorous creature he was, the Fifth Ranker raised his head from his stooped shoulders and looked over toward the speaker. It was the voice of Fujiwara no Toshihito, who at the time was the ancillary of the regent Mototsune and the son of Tokinaga, the Minister of Popular Affairs. He was a big, broad-shouldered, manly figure, much taller than average. At the moment he was eating boiled chestnuts and downing one cup of black sake after another. The sake appeared to have taken its affect. Looking at the Fifth Ranker's raised face, he added in a tone that combined sympathy and contempt, "What a sorry sight. Shall I give you enough to satisfy your heart's desire?"

A dog that is continually being abused hesitates when offered meat to eat. In equal turns the Fifth Ranker looked at the face of Toshihito and at his empty cup, his face assuming its characteristic expression between crying and laughing.

"That's not to your liking?"

"……"

"Well?"

"……"

The Fifth Ranker could feel all eyes upon him. Depending on his answer, he might again be made the object of ridicule. On the other hand, he couldn't help feel that no matter what his answer, they would make fun of him. He wasn't sure what to do. If Toshihito had indicated in his tone of voice that he found the matter altogether too much trouble and said, "If that's not to your liking, I won't insist," then the Fifth Ranker would probably have continued to divide his time between gazing at his empty bowl and Toshihito's face.

But hearing Toshihito's response, the Fifth Ranker hurriedly replied, "Oh no, I couldn't do that."

Everyone listening to the exchange between the two suddenly burst out laughing. There were even some who parroted the Fifth Ranker's reply, "Oh no, I couldn't do that." Above the various bowls of colorful citrus fruit, numerous soft and stiff hats moved like restless waves, accompanying the laughing voices. Among these voices, the one that was loudest, the one that was most cheerful of all, was Toshihito's.

"Then I will treat you to a bit of yam gruel one of these days," Tosihihito said, with a slight frown on his face. It seemed that an emerging laugh and the sake he had just drunk had gotten stuck in his throat. "All right?"

"I would be honored," the Fifth Ranker replied.

Growing red and stuttering as he spoke, he repeated how humbled he felt by the invitation. Needless to say, the whole party burst into laughter again. Toshihito, in an attempt to encourage the merrymakers, shook his broad shoulders in glee and laughed even more loudly. This rustic samurai from the north country knew only two styles of life: one was drinking, the other laughing.

Fortunately, however, the principal subject of conversation soon turned away from these two. This may have been because the outsiders among the group had grown tired of the red-nosed Fifth Ranker being the focus of attention, whether it was mockery or not. In any case, talk shifted from one thing to another, and just about the time when drinks and food had grown scarce, the whole party became intrigued by the story of a samurai university student who tried to mount a horse with both legs thrust into one side of his chaps. The Fifth Ranker, however, seemed not to hear a word the others were saying. The two words "yam gruel" seemed to occupy all his thoughts. Even when grilled pheasant was placed in front of him, he didn't pick up his chopsticks. When black sake was served, he didn't raise it to his lips. He simply sat with his hands placed on his knees, his face flushed to his temples like a naive young woman meeting a prospective marriage partner for the first time, looking longingly at the empty black-lacquer bowl, smiling childishly.

* * *

Four or five days had passed when two men could be seen proceeding leisurely on horseback down the road to Awataguchi, following the riverbed of Kamogawa river. One of them was carrying an embossed sword and wearing an indigo-blue hunting suit with the same color pleated trousers, sporting a dark mustache and handsome sideburns. The other was wearing a shabby bluish-gray informal *suikan* over two layers of thinly wadded cloth, and appeared to be around forty. From the sloppy way he tied his sash and from his runny red nose, he seemed to lack nothing in the way of shabbiness. The horses the two were riding were three year olds—the one in front cream colored, and the one behind dappled gray, both so fast of foot that peddlers and samurai along the road turned to look as they went past. Following them were two more men on foot, trying not to fall behind the horses, undoubtedly a porter and a valet.—This made up, it hardly needs saying, the party of Tosihihito and the Fifth Ranker.

Even though winter, it was a serenely fine day, and from between the rocks of the bright riverbed, near where the water was flowing, mugwort was growing, its leaves undisturbed by any breeze. The short leafless willow trees facing the river shone with amberlike droplets of sun. The treetops moved energetically like the tails of wagtails and threw their shadows on the surface of the road. Above the dark mountains of Higashiyama, on a shoulder that looked like frost-bitten velvet, was clearly Mount Hiei. In this brilliant sunlit scene the two men, astride mother-of-pearl saddles and without resorting to the use of whips, proceeded leisurely toward Awataguchi.

"Where would it be, this place you are taking me?" the Fifth Ranker inquired, holding the reins in his inexpert hands.

"It's close by. Not as far as you are thinking."

"Then it would be around Awataguchi?"

"You wouldn't be entirely wrong in thinking that."

That morning, when Toshihito came for the Fifth Ranker, he said that he knew a place with a good hot spring that they could visit, and the Fifth Ranker took him at his word. It had been a good while since he had taken a hot bath, and his whole body had been itching for some time. If he was not only treated to yam gruel but could enjoy a not bath, he couldn't imagine anything that would make him happier. So thinking, he had mounted the dapple gray that Toshihito had brought with him. However, riding abreast and having come this far, it turned out that this was not what Toshihito had in mind. In fact, before the Fifth Ranker knew it, they had passed Awataguchi.

"So it is not Awataguchi," the Fifth Ranker remarked.

"That's right. Just a little further on."

Though smiling, Toshihito intentionally turned his eyes away from the Fifth Ranker's face and continued riding easily on. Houses on both sides of the road became increasingly scarce, and the only thing that could be seen were crows searching for food in the broad winter fields. In the shadows of the mountains, the last of the snow was faintly blue, rising in mist into the air. The sky was clear, and the spiky treetops of the wax trees pierced the sky, pricking the eyes and chilling the bones.

"Then, would it be somewhere around Yamashina?"

"This is Yamashina. Just a little further ahead."

It was true. While they were talking, they had passed Yamashina. But not only that. In the meanwhile they had also passed Sekiyama, and with this and that, a little after noon they had finally arrived in front of Miidera temple. Toshihito was a close friend of one of the monks there. They called on the monk and were treated to lunch. Then they remounted their horses and hurried on their way. In comparison to the road just traveled, this one had far fewer human dwellings. In particular, it should be remembered that bandits were widespread at the time.—Pulling his stooped shoulders down lower, the Fifth Ranker looked up at Toshihito and asked:

"Not there yet?"

Toshihito smiled. It was the kind of smile that a child might give who has been caught playing a trick on an older person. The wrinkles gathered at the tip of his nose and the muscles sagging at the edge of his eyes indicated a hesitation as whether to laugh or not. Finally he said:

"To tell the truth, I am thinking of taking you to Tsuruga." Laughing aloud, he raised his whip and pointed at the far-off sky. Below the whip, shining brightly in the evening sun, was Lake Biwa.

The Fifth Ranker was dumbfounded.

"By Tsuruga you mean Tsuruga in Echizen. In Echizen...?"

It wasn't that the Fifth Ranker hadn't often heard that Toshihito lived mostly in Tsuruga since marrying the daughter of the Tsuruga native Fujiwara no Arihito. But it hadn't occurred to him until this very moment that Toshihito was taking him there. First of all, how would it be possible to get safely to Echizen province, crossing countless mountains and rivers, with a mere two attendants. Moreover, there were widespread rumors these days of travelers being murdered by bandits.—The Fifth Ranker looked Toshihito in the face as if appealing for an explanation and said under his breath:

"Come now, you must be joking! At first I understood it to be Higashiyama, but it was Yamashina. Then I understood it to be

Yamashina, but it was Miidera. In the end it's Tsuruga in Echizen. Which is it to be? If you had told me from the beginning, I could have brought the proper attendants.—But Tsuruga, how absurd!"

As the Fifth Ranker muttered to himself, his face quavered on the edge of breaking down. If it hadn't been for the thought of eating his fill of yam gruel, he might then and there have left and returned to Kyoto on his own.

"Think of me, Fujiwara no Toshihito, as being the equal of a thousand men. There is no need to worry about highwaymen."

Seeing how agitated the Fifth Ranker was, Toshihito frowned and teased him a bit. Then he called the porter to his side, got a quiver to fix on his back, and took a black-lacquered bow and placed it across his saddle. He then set off, leading the way. Given the situation, the spineless Fifth Ranker really had no choice but to blindly follow Toshihito's wishes. As the Fifth Ranker looked forlornly at the desolate plains of his surroundings, he repeatedly chanted in his head half-remember lines of the *Kannon Sutra*, his red nose virtually rubbing against the pommel of the saddle. His horse plodded on, its gait as unsteady as ever.

The horses' hooves echoed over the plain, which was profusely covered in yellowing thatching grass. In places there were puddles of water that reflected the cold blue sky, which would undoubtedly freeze with the coming of this winter's evening. On the horizon was a mountain range, which perhaps because it was facing away from the setting sun was devoid of shining patches of lingering snow, though the sky had long been painted in a dark purple. Even then, the view was obstructed by numerous thickets of bleak pampas grass, and often the two attendants lost sight of what was ahead.—Suddenly Toshihito turned to the Fifth Ranker and called out, "Look, a good messenger has arrived. Let's send a message back to Tsuruga."

The Fifth Ranker didn't immediately grasp what Toshihito meant, and he looked timidly in the direction Toshihito was pointing with his bow. This wasn't a place, in any case, where a human figure could be easily spotted, but among some shrubbery entangled with wild grapevines and such, a solitary fox was walking slowly along, warming its snug-colored coat of fur in the rays of the declining sun.—But then, suddenly, the fox leaped wildly into the air and ran off as straight as an arrow in no particular direction. The reason was that Toshihito had snapped his whip and was headed toward the fox. The Fifth Ranker, without a thought for what he was doing, followed hard on Toshihito. The two attendants, needless to say, did their best to keep up. For a while the silence of the plain was broken by the clatter of hooves' scattering rocks, but eventually Toshihito brought his horse to a halt, and it could be seen that he had managed to capture the fox, for he was holding it upside down by its back legs by the side of his saddle. The fox had run until it could run no more, and then had been trapped under the legs of Toshihito's horse and caught. The Fifth Ranker, busily wiping the sweat collecting in his thinning mustache, finally caught up with Toshihito.

"Now listen carefully, Fox," Toshihito was saying in a purposely grave tone, raising the fox up to eye level. "Tonight you will go to the Toshihito Tsuruga estate and convey the following message: 'Toshihito will soon be arriving at the estate with guests. Tomorrow, at the hour of the snake, have servants waiting at Takashima along with two saddled horses.' Got that? Now don't forget."

As he finished speaking, Toshihito swung the fox around once and then threw it into a thicket some distance away.

"God, look at him run! Look at him run!"

The two attendants, who had finally caught up, clapped their hands and cheered as they watched the fox make its getaway. The back of the fox, the color of autumn leaves in the setting sun, ran on and on straight as an arrow, in spite of the tree roots and rocks underfoot. From where the group stood, they could see the scene as plain as day. This was due to the fact that in chasing the fox, they had somehow emerged at a high point where the gentle slope of the plain merged with the dry riverbed.

"It seems you have chosen a remarkable messenger, I must say."

As the Fifth Ranker let slip these words of naive respect and admiration for this rustic samurai who could even make use of foxes as messengers, he looked up at Toshihito's face as if seeing him for the first time. He didn't have the time to consider the gap that lay between them. Yet he found it reassuring that his will was encompassed within the broader scope of Toshihito's will and that it had consequently come to exercise a greater degree of freedom.—Flattery most likely comes naturally into being in times like this. If the reader should hereafter discover in the Fifth Ranker's behavior something resembling a fawning jester, he should not on the basis of that alone rashly question the character of this man.

After being thrown through the air, the fox ran down the sloping surface almost as if tumbling headlong down a hill, cleverly leaping lickety-split over the rocks in the dry riverbed. Then he rushed crossways up the opposite bank. As he was doing so, he looked back and saw the group of samurai who had caught him as it gathered on the slope in the far distance, their horses standing side by side. They looked small, about the size of fingers being held up in a line. Especially the cream-colored and dappled-gray horses stood out in the westering sun more clearly in the frost-filled air than if they had been drawn with a brush.

The fox then turned around and began running again as fast as the wind through the dried pampas grass.

* * *

The next day, exactly at the hour of the snake, Toshihito's party arrived at Takashima according to plan. Takashima was a modest village facing Biwako Lake. Unlike yesterday the sky was clouded over. Under it were a number of thatched houses scattered here and there. Between the pine trees growing along the shore could be seen gray ripples approaching the land. The surface of the water, which had all the appearance of an unpolished mirror, looked cold and uninviting. —Having come this far, Toshihito looked back at the Fifth Ranker and said:

"Just look. The men have come, just as I said."

And looking, the Fifth Ranker saw twenty or thirty men leading two saddled horses, some of the men mounted and some on foot. The sleeves of their *suikan* flapping in the cold wind, they came from the shores of the lake, from between the pine trees, hurrying toward the newly arrived party. When they drew near, the men on horses quickly dismounted and those on foot kneeled at the side of the road, both waiting respectfully for the approach of Toshihito.

"It seems the fox fulfilled his job as a messenger."

"For creatures with the innate ability to transform themselves, that is a simple feat."

As Toshihito and the Fifth Ranker were conversing in this way, they reached the spot where Toshihito's vassals were waiting. Toshihito called out, "I'm much obliged." The kneeling men quickly stood and took the horses' bridles. Suddenly the atmosphere became very cheerful.

"Something unusual happened last night."

Toshihito was addressed thus after he and the Fifth Ranker had dismounted and almost before they had assumed their seats of honor. The speaker was a gray-hair vassal in a dark-red *suikan* who approached Toshihito as he spoke. Toshihito readily answered, "And what would that be?" as his vassals served him food and drinks and he encouraged the Fifth Ranker to share in the meal.

"By your leave, sire. Last night, about the hour of the dog, the lady of the house suddenly lost consciousness. She said, 'I am the fox from Sakamoto. Today I was given a message from your lord, so draw near and listen carefully.' All present gathered before her, and she uttered these words: 'The lord is preparing to leave for the estate immediately with a guest. Tomorrow, about the time of the snake, send men to meet me at Takashima with two saddled horses.' She spoke in this way."

"That is truly something extraordinary," the Fifth Ranker said in agreement, looking meaningfully at the faces of Toshihito and his vassals and attempting to give a response that would satisfy both. "And it was not just what she said, the old vassal added; she was so afraid that she was shaking like a leaf. 'They can't be late. If they are late, I'll be disowned by his lord,' she said, crying without letup."

"What happened after that?"

"After that she peacefully retired to rest, the old man said. When we went in and out of her room, she never woke."

"Well, what do you think?" Toshihito asked the Fifth Ranker somewhat proudly when the elderly vassal had finished speaking. "Even animals do my bidding."

"I am absolutely amazed," replied the Fifth Ranker as he scratched his red nose and lowered his head in a slight bow, purposely leaving his mouth gaping opened to show how astonished he was. His mustache sported droplets of the sake he had been drinking.

* * *

It was the night of the same day. In a room in Toshihito's estate the Fifth Ranker, unable to sleep, gazed with bleary eyes at the light of the lamp throughout the night. Various images of the trip there this evening came successively to his mind—the friendly talk with Toshihito and his servants, the passage over hills covered with pine trees, over creeks and dry plains, as well as through grass, tree leaves, rocks, and the smell of smoke from the burning of fields. Especially when they had finally reached the estate in the dusky haze of twilight and seen the red charcoal flames of the long brazier, he had felt an immense sense of relief. Now, in bed, it all seemed like something that had happened long ago. The Fifth Ranker stretched out his legs under a luxurious, well-wadded yellow robe and absently surveyed himself and his surroundings.

Under the robe that Toshihito had lent him the Fifth Ranker wore two thickly wadded yellowish-white silk undergarments. That alone could warm him enough to make him break out in a sweat, but in addition to that, the alcohol consumed at dinner had taken its effect. Just beyond the latticed shutters by his pillow was a large frost-covered garden, but that didn't bother him in his mellow mood. It was all so completely different from his quarters in the capital. Still, there was a disharmony in his heart that made him uneasy. First, time seemed to be passing so slowly. The coming of the dawn—the time when he could eat yam gruel—could not, he felt, come soon enough. After the clash of these two emotions, the feeling of unease resulting from the sudden change in situation would lead to a chilling pall much like today's weather. All of this, despite the warmth, would prevent him from falling easily to sleep.

It was then that the loud voice of someone in the garden struck the Fifth Ranker's ears. Judging from the sound, it was the gray-haired elder who had come to meet them halfway, and who was now making an announcement.

Perhaps it was because his gravelly voice rang out against the frost, but each word struck the Fifth Ranker to the bone like the first frigid wind of winter.

"Listen up, all servants. The lord instructs each of you to bring one mountain yam, 9 centimeters wide and 152 centimeters long, by the hour of the rabbit tomorrow morning. By the hour of the rabbit, you hear. Don't forget."

This was repeated two or three times, and then, all of a sudden, all signs of human life vanished, and in an instant the quiet winter night reverted to its original form. In the ensuing silence the only sounds to be heard were those emitted by the burning oil lamp, whose red flame wavered and swayed like burning floss. The Fifth Ranker stifled a yawn and sank once again into thought.—By giving instructions for mountain yams to be collected, the idea was surely to make yam gruel. So thinking, he had forgotten for a moment the earlier feeling of uneasiness by focusing his attention outside himself, but now the feeling of unease resurfaced in his mind. In particular, what was stronger than before was the thought that he didn't want to acquire the yam gruel too easily; this mean-spirited notion lay unmovably at the core of his thoughts. Now that it seemed that partaking of yam gruel would become a reality, it also appeared that all the years he had patiently awaited this moment had been for nothing. If it were possible, he would prefer that some incident occurred that prevented him from partaking of the gruel, or that the incident was resolved enabling him now to acquire the gruel, and that by some such process everything would turn out all right.—Eventually, while this thought was spinning around in his mind like a top, the Fifth Ranker fell sound asleep, exhausted from his travels.

When he woke the next morning, he immediately recalled last night's incident involving the mountain yams and raised the latticed shutters to look outside. It appeared he had overslept and the hour of the rabbit had come and gone. Out in the garden four or five large straw mats had been laid out, on which there were some two or three thousand loglike objects piled up almost as high as the slanting eves of the cypress-thatched roof. Looking closer, he could see that they were gargantuan mountain yams, 9 centimeters in diameter and 1.5 meters in height.

Rubbing his sleepy eyes, the Fifth Ranker looked dizzily around with an astonishment that verged on panic. There were five or six cauldrons resting side by side on what were apparently newly driven piles. There were dozens of maidservants in indigo-blue garments working busily around them. Some were tending the fires, some were sweeping up the ashes, some were pouring the sweetener called *amazuramisen* from unpainted wooden tubs into the cauldrons. All were busy as bees preparing to make yam gruel. As the smoke coming from the bottom of the cauldrons and the steam rising from inside them joined with the lingering morning mist, all the objects in the garden assumed a blurry appearance. In this enveloping grayness, the only bit of red was the intensely burning fire under the cauldrons. In both sight and sound, it was as if he were caught in the midst of the clamor of a battle scene or the commotion of a terrible accident. Now, as if for the first time, the Fifth Ranker considered the fact that these prodigious mountain yams would turn into yam gruel in these huge cauldrons. He also considered the fact that he had traveled all the way from Kyoto to Tsuruga in Echizen to partake of this yam gruel. The more he thought about it, the more he felt the meaningless of it all. The fact was, his long-held appetite for yam gruel was now half gone.

One hour later the Fifth Ranker, Toshihito, and Toshihito's father-in-law, Arihito, were sitting down for breakfast. In front of each was a silver decanter brimming with nearly 18 awesome liters of yam gruel.

Earlier the Fifth Ranker had seen dozens of energetic young men deftly wielding thin kitchen knives to slice the yams that had been piled up to the height of the eaves. He had watched as the maidservants bustled about, scraping up every bit of yam and depositing it in the cauldrons, repeatedly scraping and depositing. Finally, as the last yam had disappeared from the mats on which they had been lying, several plumes of steam imbued with the aroma of the yams and *amazura* rose from the cauldrons with the wind into the clear morning sky. Having seen all this, it was perhaps not surprising that the Fifth Ranker, when face to face with a decanter, should already feel stuffed before touching a bit of the gruel to his lips.—He wiped the sweat from his forehead, feeling the ill-timed nature of his reaction.

"You can't have had your fill yet. Please help yourself to more."

Toshihito's father-in-law, Arihito, instructed some children to bring more silver cauldrons. Each was filled with gruel to overflowing. Closing his eyes, and with his red nose growing redder still, he poured almost half of a decanter into a large earthen bowl and drank it down unwillingly.

"Father wants you to drink up. Don't hesitate out of modesty."

With a wicked grin on his face, Toshihito spoke up from the side, pressing the Fifth

Ranker to have another decanter. Far from being modest, another bowl of gruel was the farthest thing from the Fifth Ranker's mind. Even now he had barely managed to finish off half a decanter. If he had any more than this, it would likely come back up before it cleared his throat. But if he didn't drink anymore, it would be equivalent to spurning Toshihito's and Arihito's kindness. Closing his eyes again he forced down half of the remaining one-third. The rest was beyond him, even a single mouthful.

"Oh, yes. I'm infinitely obliged. Having had more than enough.—Goodness, yes, infinitely obliged," said the Fifth Ranker a little incoherently. But what gave him an even more disoriented look was the fact that, even though it was winter, there were beads of sweat dangling from his mustache and nose.

"What a small eater! Our guest is holding

back, it seems. Hey, you over there, what are you doing?"

Attending to Arihito's words, the children began to fill another earthen cup with gruel from a decanter. The Fifth Ranker raised both hands as if to ward off a fly and indicated that he would like to be excused.

"Oh, no. I have had more than enough. You will have to pardon me, but I have had more than enough."

At this point, if Toshihito had not pointed to a house across the way and suddenly said, "Look at that!" Arihito would probably have continued urging the Fifth Ranker to eat more yam gruel. Fortunately, however, this directed everyone's attention to the cypress-thatched house Toshihito was pointing at. The morning sun was then shining brightly on the eves of the house. Sitting there in the dazzling light, quietly grooming its lustrous fur, sat a fox. A close look revealed that it was the same fox that Toshihito had caught on the dry plain two days ago. It was the fox from Sakamoto.

"The fox has apparently visited us for some yam gruel. You there, give it some gruel to eat."

Toshihito's orders were quickly carried out. And the fox, jumping down from the eves, immediately helped itself to the yam in the big garden.

The Fifth Ranker, watching the fox eat, nostalgically reflected back on the image of himself before he came here. It was a time when many samurai had ridiculed him. A time when even Kyoto kids mocked him, saying, "What do you want, Red Nose?" A time when he had wandered Suzaku Avenue in his faded *suikan* and *sashinuki* like a stray shaggy mutt, pitiful and alone. But it was also a time when he was happy, clinging alone to his long-held desire to eat yam gruel.—He felt a sense of relief that he would no longer have to worry about eating yam gruel, and almost at the same moment he felt the sweat on his face drop from his nose and slowly dry up. It was a very fine morning in Tsuruga, but the wind was bitterly cold. Suddenly the Fifth Ranker grasped his nose, and facing the direction of the silver decanters, he let out a stupendous sneeze.

Word List

・本文で使われている全ての語を掲載しています（LEVEL 1、2）。ただし、LEVEL 3以上は、中学校レベルの語を含みません。

・語形が規則変化する語の見出しは原形で示しています。不規則変化語は本文中で使われている形になっています。

・一般的な意味を紹介していますので、一部の語で本文で実際に使われている品詞や意味と合っていないことがあります。

・品詞は以下のように示しています。

名 名詞	代 代名詞	形 形容詞	副 副詞	動 動詞	助 助動詞
前 前置詞	接 接続詞	間 間投詞	冠 冠詞	略 略語	俗 俗語
頭 接頭語	尾 接尾語	号 記号	関 関係代名詞		

A B C D E F G H I J K L M N O P Q R S T U V W X Y Z

A

□ **abalone** 名 アワビ

□ **abandoned** 動 abandon（捨てる）の過去，過去分詞 形 ①見捨てられた，放棄された ②気ままな

□ **ability** 名 ①できること，（～する）能力 ②才能

□ **about** 熟 **come about** 起こる **worry about** ～のことを心配する

□ **abreast** 副（横に）並んで

□ **abruptly** 副 不意に，突然，急に

□ **absently** 副 ぼんやりと，上の空で

□ **absolutely** 副 ①完全に，確実に ②《yesを強調する返事として》そうですとも

□ **absurd** 形 常識に反した，ばかげた

□ **abuse** 動 虐待する，悪用する 名 虐待，悪用，乱用

□ **accident** 名 ①（不慮の）事故，災難 ②偶然

□ **accompany** 動 ①ついていく，つきそう ②（～に）ともなって起こる ③伴奏をする

□ **accomplished** 動 accomplish（成し遂げる）の過去・過去分詞 形 ①完成した ②（技量に）優れた，熟達した

□ **according** 副《– to ～》～によれば［よると］

□ **acquire** 動 ①（努力して）獲得する，確保する ②（学力，技術などを）習得する

□ **act** 名 行為，行い 動 ①行動する ②機能する ③演じる

□ **Adam's apple** 喉仏

□ **add** 動 ①加える，足す ②足し算をする ③言い添える

□ **addition** 名 ①付加，追加，添加 ②足し算 **in addition to** ～に加えて，さらに

□ **address** 名 ①住所，アドレス ②演説 動 ①あて名を書く ②演説をする，話しかける

□ **admiration** 名 賞賛（の的），感嘆

□ **adopted** 形 ①養子［養女］になった ②採用された

□ **advance** 名 進歩，前進

□ **advantage** 名 有利な点［立場］，強み，優越 **take advantage of** ～を利用する，～につけ込む

□ **advisor** 名 忠告者，助言者，顧問

□ **afar** 副 遠くに，遠く 名 遠方

□ **affair** 名 ①事柄，事件 ②《-s》業務，仕事，やるべきこと

□ **affect** 動 ①影響する ②（病気などが）おかす ③ふりをする 名 感情，欲望

□ **affirm** 動 断言する，肯定する

□ **afford** 動《can –》～することができる，～する（経済的・時間的な）余裕がある

□ **after that** その後

□ **agitated** 形 ①かき乱された ②興奮した 動 agitateの過去，過去分詞

□ **aglow** 形〔赤く〕輝いて

□ **ago** 熟 **long ago** ずっと前に，昔

□ **agreement** 名 ①合意，協定 ②一致

□ **albeit** 接 ～にもかかわらず

□ **alcohol** 名 アルコール

□ **all** 熟 **all of a sudden** 突然，前触れもなしに **all right** 大丈夫で，申し分ない，承知した **all the way** ずっと，はるばる **first of all** まず第一に **with all** ～がありながら

□ **along** 熟 **along with** ～と一緒に **shuffle along** 足を引きずって歩く，すり足で歩く **walk along**（前へ）歩く，～に沿って歩く

□ **aloud** 副 大声で，（聞こえるように）声を出して

□ **altogether** 副 まったく，全然，全部で 名 全体

□ **amazed** 動 amaze（びっくりさせる）の過去，過去分詞 形 びっくりした，驚いた

□ **amazura** 名 甘葛（あまづら）《一般的には，ブドウ科のツル性植物のこと。また，その樹液を煮詰めて作られる甘味料のひとつ》

□ **amazuramisen** 名 甘葛未煎（あまづらみせん）《甘葛から採れる樹液》

□ **amberlike** 形 飴色の，琥珀色の

□ **amid** 前 ～の間で，～の最中に

□ **amount** 名 ①量，額 ②《the –》合計 動（総計～に）なる

□ **ancient** 形 昔の，古代の

□ **ancillary** 名 補助者，助手，恪勤（かくごん）《平安時代，院・親王家・大臣家などに仕えた武士》

□ **and so** そこで，それだから

□ **angry** 熟 **get angry** 腹を立てる

□ **announcement** 名 発表，アナウンス，告示，声明

□ **any** 熟 **in any case** とにかく

□ **anymore** 副《通例否定文，疑問文で》今はもう，これ以上，これから

□ **anyone** 代 ①《疑問文・条件節で》誰か ②《否定文で》誰も（～ない） ③《肯定文で》誰でも

□ **anywhere** 副 どこかへ［に］，どこにも，どこへも，どこにでも

□ **apparently** 副 見たところ～らしい，明らかに

□ **appealing** 形〔表情などが〕訴える［哀願する］ような

□ **appear** 動 ①現れる，見えてくる ②（～のように）見える，～らしい **appear to** ～するように見える

□ **appearance** 名 ①現れること，出現 ②外見，印象

□ **appetite** 名 ①食欲 ②欲求

□ **appraise** 動 鑑定する，値踏みする

□ **approach** 動 ①接近する ②話を持ちかける 名 接近，（～へ）近づく道

□ **appropriate** 形 ①適切な，ふさわしい，妥当な ②特殊な，特有の 動 ①割り当てる ②自分のものにする，占有する

□ **aroma** 名 ①香り，におい，芳香 ②（芸術品などの）気品，風格

□ **around** 熟 **turn around** 振り向く，向きを変える

□ **arrive at** ～に着く

□ **arrow** 名 矢，矢のようなもの

□ **as best one can** 精一杯，できるだけ

□ **as far as** ～と同じくらい遠く，～まで，～する限り（では）

□ **as for** ～に関しては，～はどうかと言うと

□ **as if** あたかも～のように，まるで～みたいに

□ **as well as** ～と同様に

□ **as ～ as ever** 相変わらず，これまでのように

□ **as ～ as one can** できる限り～

□ **as ～ as possible** できるだけ～

□ **ascend** 動〔階段や坂などを〕登る，上がる

□ **ash** 名 ①灰，燃えかす ②《-es》遺骨，なきがら

□ **aside** 副 わきへ（に），離れて

□ **asleep** 形 眠って（いる状態の） 副 眠って，休止して

□ **assume** 動 ①仮定する，当然のことと思う ②引き受ける

□ **astonish** 動 驚かせる，びっくりさせる

□ **astonishment** 名 驚き

□ **astound** 動 仰天させる，驚かせる

□ **astride** 副 またがって

□ **at a loss** 途方に暮れて

□ **at a time** 一度に，続けざまに

□ **at first** 最初は，初めのうちは

□ **at least** 少なくとも

□ **at the moment** 今は

□ **at the time** そのころ，当時は

□ **at this point** 現在のところ

□ **at this time** 現時点では，このとき

□ **atmosphere** 名 ①大気，空気 ②雰囲気

□ **attempt** 動 試みる，企てる 名 試み，企て，努力

□ **attend** 動 ①出席する ②世話をする，仕える ③伴う ④《－to ～》～に注意を払う，専念する，～の世話をする

□ **attendant** 形 つき添いの，伴う 名 つき添い人，案内係，アテンダント

□ **attention** 名 ①注意，集中 ②配慮，手当て，世話 間《号令として》気をつけ

□ **attract** 動 ①引きつける，引く ②魅力がある，魅了する

□ **author** 名 著者，作家 動 著作する，創作する

□ **avenue** 名 ①並木道 ②《A-, Ave.》～通り，～街

□ **average** 名 平均（値），並み 形 平均の，普通の 動 平均して～になる

□ **await** 動 待つ，待ち受ける

□ **aware** 形 ①気がついて，知って ②（～の）認識のある

□ **Awataguchi** 名 粟田口《地名》

□ **away** 熟 **turn away** 向こうへ行く，それる，（顔を）そむける

□ **awesome** 形 ①畏敬の念を抱かせる ②すばらしい，見事な

□ **awkwardness** 名 ①不器用さ，ぎこちなさ ②気まずさ，居心地の悪さ

B

□ **back** 熟 **come back** 戻る **hold back**（感情を）抑える，自制する **look back at** ～に視線を戻す，～を振り返って見る **push back** 押し返す，押しのける **step back** 後ずさりする，後に下がる

□ **backbone** 名 ①背骨 ②主力，中心

□ **background** 名 背景，前歴，生い立ち

□ **badger** 名 アナグマ

□ **ballooning-trousers** 名 裾の膨らんだズボン（＝指貫，さしぬき）

□ **bamboo** 名 竹（類），竹材 形 竹の

□ **bandit** 名 強盗，追いはぎ，山賊

□ **banquet** 名 宴会，ごちそう

□ **bar** 名 ①酒場 ②棒, かんぬき ③障害(物) 動 かんぬきで閉める

□ **barely** 副 ①かろうじて, やっと ②ほぼ, もう少しで

□ **base** 名 基礎, 土台, 本部 動《– on ～》～に基礎を置く, 基づく

□ **basic** 形 基礎の, 基本の 名《-s》基礎, 基本, 必需品

□ **basically** 副 基本的には, 大筋では

□ **basis** 名 ①土台, 基礎 ②基準, 原理 ③根拠 ④主成分

□ **battle** 名 戦闘, 戦い 動 戦う

□ **bead** 数珠玉,《-s》ビーズ［のネックレス］

□ **beard** 名 あごひげ

□ **beat** 動 ①打つ, 鼓動する ②打ち負かす 名 打つこと, 鼓動, 拍

□ **because of** ～のために, ～の理由で

□ **bee** 名 ミツバチ

□ **beginning** 動 begin（始まる）の現在分詞 名 初め, 始まり

□ **behavior** 名 振る舞い, 態度, 行動

□ **behind** 前 ①～の後ろに, ～の背後に ②～に遅れて, ～に劣って 副 ①後ろに, 背後に ②遅れて, 劣って **fall behind** 取り残される, 後れを取る

□ **being** 動 be（～である）の現在分詞 名 存在, 生命, 人間 **human being** 人, 人間

□ **below** 前 ①～より下に ②～以下の, ～より劣る 副 下に［へ］

□ **beneath** 前 ～の下に［の］, ～より低い 副 下に, 劣って

□ **beside** 前 ①～のそばに, ～と並んで ②～と比べると ③～とはずれて

□ **best** 熟 **as best one can** 精一杯, できるだけ **do one's best** 全力を尽くす

□ **betto** 名 別当（べっとう）《親王家・摂関家などの政所・侍所の長官》

□ **between A and B** AとBの間に

□ **beyond** 前 ～を越えて, ～の向こうに 副 向こうに

□ **bidding** 名〔人の〕命令, 指示

□ **bind** 動 ①縛る, 結ぶ ②束縛する, 義務づける

□ **bit** 動 bite（かむ）の過去, 過去分詞 名 ①小片, 少量 ②《a –》少し, ちょっと **bit of**《a –》少しの～, ちょっとした～

□ **bitterly** 副 激しく, 苦々しく

□ **Biwako Lake** 琵琶湖

□ **black-lacquer** 名 黒漆塗り（の）

□ **black-lacquered** 形 黒漆塗りの

□ **blade** 名（刀・ナイフなどの）刃

□ **bleak** 形 荒涼とした, わびしい

□ **bleary** 形〔目が〕かすんだ, ぼんやりした

□ **blindly** 副〔命令・助言・権力などに従うことが〕無思慮に, よく考えもせず, 無分別に

□ **blown** 動 blow（吹く）の過去分詞

□ **bluish-gray** 形 青みがかった灰色の

□ **blurry** 形 ①しみだらけの ②ぼやけた

□ **boast** 動 自慢する, 誇る, 鼻にかける 名 自慢（話）, 誇り

□ **boil** 動 ①沸騰する［させる］, 煮える, 煮る ②激高する 名 沸騰

□ **bone** 名 ①骨,《-s》骨格 ②《-s》要点, 骨組み 動（魚・肉）の骨をとる

□ **born into**《be –》～に生まれる

□ **both A and B** AもBも

□ **bother** 動 悩ます, 困惑させる 名 面倒, いざこざ, 悩みの種

□ **bottom** 名 ①底, 下部, すそ野, ふもと, 最下位, 根底 ②尻 形 底の, 根底の

□ **bow** 動（～に）お辞儀する 名 ①お辞儀, えしゃく ②弓, 弓状のもの

□ **braided** 形 ①組みひも［リボン］で飾った ②〔3本以上のひもで〕編んだ

□ **brazier** 名〔暖房用の〕火鉢，火桶

□ **break out in** 〔発熱・不安感などで汗が〕出る

□ **break up** ばらばらになる

□ **bream** 名《sea –》タイ科の魚

□ **breath** 名 ①息，呼吸 ②《a –》（風の）そよぎ，気配，きざし

□ **breathing** 動 breathe（呼吸する）の現在分詞 名 ①呼吸，息づかい ②《a –》ひと息の間，ちょっとの間

□ **breathlessly** 副 ハラハラしながら，息を切らして

□ **breeze** 名 そよ風 動（風が）そよそよと吹く

□ **bridle** 名 馬勒《頭部馬具。おもがい・くつわ・手綱》

□ **brightly** 副 明るく，輝いて，快活に

□ **brilliant** 形 光り輝く，見事な，すばらしい

□ **brim** 名（容器の）縁，（帽子の）つば 動 縁までいっぱいになる

□ **bring up** （問題を）持ち出す

□ **broad** 形 ①幅の広い ②寛大な ③明白な 副 すっかり，十分に

□ **broad-shouldered** 形 肩幅の広い

□ **Buddhist** 形 仏教（徒）の，仏陀の 名 仏教徒

□ **bully** 動 いじめる，おどす 名 いじめっ子

□ **bullying** 名 弱い者いじめ

□ **burning** 動 burn（燃える）の現在分詞 形 ①燃えている，燃えるように暑い ②のどが渇いた，激しい

□ **burst** 動 ①爆発する［させる］ ②破裂する［させる］ **burst into** 急に～する **burst out laughing** 爆笑する **burst out ～ing** 急に～し出す 名 ①破裂，爆発 ②突発

□ **busily** 副 忙しく，せっせと

□ **bustle** 動 ①忙しく［せかせか］動く ②せき立てる 名 せわしげな動き

□ **butt** 名 ①尻 ②（たばこの）吸いさし ③物笑いの種になる人 ④（武器・道具の）大きいほうの端 動 ①干渉する，口を出す ②頭で突く

□ **by the side of** ～のそばに

□ **bystander** 名 傍観者，見物人

C

□ **call on** 訪問する

□ **call out** 叫ぶ，呼び出す，声を掛ける

□ **call to** ～に声をかける

□ **can** 熟 **as best one can** 精一杯，できるだけ **as ～ as one can** できる限り～

□ **can't help (but)** ～せずにはいられない

□ **cannon** 名 大砲

□ **cannot help ～ing** ～せずにはいられない

□ **capital** 名 首都

□ **capture** 動 捕える 名 捕えること，捕獲（物）

□ **carriage** 名 ①馬車 ②乗り物，車

□ **carry out** 外へ運び出す，［計画を］実行する

□ **case** 熟 **in any case** とにかく

□ **casually** 副 何気なく，軽い気持ちで，偶然に

□ **catch on** ～を捕まえる

□ **catch up with** ～に追いつく

□ **cauldron** 名 大釜

□ **cautiously** 副 用心して，慎重に

□ **caw** 名〔カラスなどの〕カーという声 動〔カラスなどが〕カーカーと鳴く

□ **cease** 動やむ，やめる，中止する 名終止

□ **ceiling** 名 ①天井 ②上限，最高価格

□ **centimeter** 名センチメートル《長さの単位》

□ **certain** 形 ①確実な，必ず～する ②(人が)確信した ③ある ④いくらかの 代(～の中の)いくつか

□ **chant** 名さえずり 動詠唱する

□ **chap** 名 ①あかぎれ ②やつ，男

□ **character** 名 ①特性，個性 ②品性，人格

□ **characteristic** 形特徴のある，独特の 名特徴，特性，特色，持ち味

□ **charcoal** 名木炭

□ **chase** 動 ①追跡する，追い[探し]求める ②追い立てる

□ **chat** 動おしゃべりをする，談笑する

□ **cheek** 名ほお

□ **cheerful** 形上機嫌の，元気のよい，(人を)気持ちよくさせる

□ **chest** 名 ①大きな箱，戸棚，たんす ②金庫 ③胸，肺

□ **chestnut** 名クリ(栗) 形栗色の，栗毛の

□ **chew** 動 ①かむ ②じっくり考える 名かむこと，そしゃく

□ **childish** 形子どもっぽい，幼稚な

□ **childishly** 副〈侮蔑的〉〔大人が〕子どもみたいに

□ **chill** 動 ①冷やす ②寒がらせる 名冷え，身にしみる寒さ

□ **chilly** 形 ①冷え冷えする，ぞくぞくする ②冷淡な

□ **chilly-looking** 形寒そうな

□ **choice** 名選択(の範囲・自由)，えり好み，選ばれた人[物] **have no choice but to** ～するしかない 形精選した

□ **chopstick** 名《ふつう -s》はし

□ **circle** 名 ①円，円周，輪 ②循環，軌道 ③仲間，サークル 動回る，囲む

□ **citrus** 名《植物》かんきつ類 形《植物》かんきつ類の[に関する]

□ **clamor** 名騒がしい音，騒ぎ立てる声 動騒ぎ立てる

□ **clap** 動(手を)たたく

□ **clash** 動 ①(意見，利害が)衝突する ②(金属同士がぶつかって)ガチャンと鳴る 名(意見，利害の)衝突

□ **clatter** 名がたがたいう音 動がたがた音を立てる

□ **clay** 名粘土，白土

□ **clear** 形 ①はっきりした，明白な ②澄んだ ③(よく)晴れた 動 ①はっきりさせる ②片づける ③晴れる 副 ①はっきりと ②すっかり，完全に

□ **clearly** 副 ①明らかに，はっきりと ②《返答に用いて》そのとおり

□ **cleverly** 副 ①利口に，賢く，巧妙に ②器用に，上手に

□ **cling** 動くっつく，しがみつく，執着する

□ **close by** すぐ近くに

□ **clothe** 動服を着せる，《受け身形で》(～を)着ている，(～の)格好をする

□ **clothing** 動clothe(服を着せる)の現在分詞 名衣類，衣料品

□ **clung** 動cling(くっつく)の過去，過去分詞

□ **cobweb** 名クモの巣

□ **coldly** 副冷たく，よそよそしく

□ **coldness** 名冷淡，冷ややかさ

□ **colored** 動color(色をつける)の過去，過去分詞 形 ①色のついた ②有色人種の，黒人の

□ **colorful** 形 ①カラフルな，派手な ②生き生きとした

□ **column** 名 ①コラム ②(新聞などの)縦の段[行・列] ③(円)柱

□ **combine** 動 ①結合する[させる]

②連合する，協力する 名合同，連合
□ **come about** 起こる
□ **come back** 戻る
□ **come down** 下りて来る
□ **come down to** ～に伝わる，～に及ぶ
□ **come for** ～に向かって来る，～を呼びに来る
□ **come into** ～の状態になる
□ **come out** 出てくる，抜ける
□ **comfort** 名①快適さ，満足 ②慰め ③安楽 動心地よくする，ほっとさせる，慰める
□ **coming** 動come（来る）の現在分詞 形今度の，来たるべき 名到来，来ること
□ **commonplace** 名平凡なこと，ありふれたもの 形平凡な，普通の，ありふれた
□ **commotion** 名①激動 ②騒動，騒ぎ
□ **communicate** 動①知らせる，連絡する ②理解し合う
□ **comparison** 名比較，対照
□ **completely** 副完全に，すっかり
□ **complexion** 名①顔色，顔貌 ②外観，様子，態度
□ **conclude** 動①終える，完結する ②結論を下す
□ **condition** 名①（健康）状態，境遇 ②《-s》状況，様子 ③条件 動適応させる，条件づける
□ **confine** 動制限する，閉じ込める
□ **confirm** 動確かめる，確かにする
□ **confront** 動①直面する，立ち向かう ②突き合わせる，比較する
□ **conscious** 形①（状況などを）意識している，自覚している ②意識のある 名意識
□ **consciousness** 名意識，自覚，気づいていること
□ **consequently** 副したがって，結果として
□ **consider** 動①考慮する，～しようと思う ②（～と）みなす ③気にかける，思いやる
□ **consideration** 名①考慮，考察 ②考慮すべきこと
□ **consist** 動①《－of ～》（部分・要素から）成る ②《－in ～》～に存在する，～にある
□ **consumed** 動consume（消費する）の過去形
□ **contemplate** 動①熟考する，よく検討する ②じっと見つめる
□ **contempt** 名軽蔑，侮辱，軽視
□ **continually** 副継続的に，絶えず，ひっきりなしに
□ **conversation** 名会話，会談
□ **converse** 動（打ち解けて）話す，会話する 名①談話 ②正反対，逆 形逆の，正反対の
□ **convey** 動①運ぶ ②伝達する，伝える ③譲渡する
□ **cord** 名ひも，コード
□ **core** 名核心，中心，芯
□ **corpse** 名（人間の）死体，死骸
□ **could have done** ～だったかもしれない《仮定法》
□ **countless** 形無数の，数え切れない
□ **courage** 名勇気，度胸
□ **course** 熟**of course** もちろん，当然
□ **courtly** 形宮廷風の，優雅な
□ **cover** 動①覆う，包む，隠す ②扱う，（～に）わたる，及ぶ ③代わりを務める ④補う 名覆い，カバー
□ **coward** 名臆病者 形勇気のない，臆病な
□ **crack** 名①割れ目，ひび ②（裂けるような）鋭い音 動①ひびが入る，ひびを入れる，割れる，割る ②鈍い音を出す

□ **crawl** 動はう，腹ばいで進む，ゆっくり進む

□ **cream** 名クリーム 形クリーム(入り)の，クリーム色の

□ **cream-colored** 形クリーム色の，淡黄色の

□ **create** 動創造する，生み出す，引き起こす

□ **creature** 名(神の)創造物，生物，動物

□ **creek** 名①小川 ②入り江

□ **cricket** 名コオロギ，キリギリス

□ **croak** 動①〔カエルが〕ゲロゲロ鳴く ②〔カラスなどが〕カーカー鳴く ③低いしわがれ声を出す

□ **crossing** 動cross(横切る)の過去，過去分詞 名横断，交差点，横断歩道，踏み切り

□ **crossway** 名交差路，交差点

□ **crouch** 動しゃがむ，うずくまる 名しゃがむこと

□ **crow** 名カラス(烏)

□ **crown** 名①冠 ②《the –》王位 ③頂，頂上 動戴冠する［させる］

□ **Crown Prince** 皇太子，親王

□ **crumble** 動①〔物が〕粉々に砕ける ②〔国・組織などが〕崩壊する ③〔計画などが〕崩れ去る

□ **curiosity** 名①好奇心 ②珍しい物［存在］

□ **custody** 名①管理，(未成年者の)保護，監督 ②監禁，留置

□ **customarily** 副通例，習慣的に

□ **cypress-thatched** 形檜皮葺(ひわだぶき)の

D

□ **daily** 形毎日の，日常の 副毎日，日ごとに 名《-lies》日刊新聞

□ **dangle** 動ぶら下がる，ぶら下げる 名ぶら下がっているもの，ぶらぶらするもの

□ **dapple** 名①〔動物の体表の〕斑点，まだら ②斑点［まだら］のある動物 形〔動物の体表が〕斑点［まだら］の 動まだらになる［する］

□ **dappled-gray** 形灰色に黒っぽい斑紋のある(馬)，葦毛の

□ **dark-blue** 形濃青色の，紺色の

□ **dark-red** 形暗い赤色の，えんじ色の

□ **darken** 動暗くする［なる］

□ **dawn** 名①夜明け ②《the –》初め，きざし 動①(夜が)明ける ②(真実などが)わかり始める

□ **day** 熟 **one day** (過去の)ある日，(未来の)いつか **one of these days** いずれそのうちに，近日中に **one of these days** 近日中に，近いうちに **these days** このごろ

□ **daytime** 名昼間

□ **dazzling** 形〔目がくらむほど〕非常に明るい，まばゆいばかりの

□ **deal** 動①分配する ②《– with [in] 〜》〜を扱う 名①取引，扱い ②(不特定の)量，額 **a good [great] deal (of 〜)** かなり［ずいぶん・大量］(の〜)，多額(の〜)

□ **death** 名①死，死ぬこと ②《the –》終えん，消滅 **to death** 死ぬまで，死ぬほど

□ **decanter** 名提(ひさげ)《銀・錫製などの，鉉(つる)と注ぎ口のある小鍋形の銚子》

□ **decline** 動①断る ②傾く ③衰える 名①傾くこと ②下り坂，衰え，衰退

□ **decompose** 動①腐敗・腐食する［させる］ ②分解する

□ **decorative** 形装飾的な，装飾用の

□ **deem** 動(〜であると)考える

□ **deftly** 副器用に，手際よく，巧みに

□ **degrade** 動 ①(地位・価値・品質などが)下がる ②退化する ③分解する ④悪化させる ⑤評判をおとしめる

□ **degree** 名 ①程度, 階級, 位, 身分 ②(温度・角度の)度

□ **delicacy** 名 ①繊細さ, 優美さ ②扱いにくさ

□ **delight** 動 喜ぶ, 喜ばす, 楽しむ, 楽しませる 名 喜び, 愉快

□ **depend** 動《– on [upon] ～》①～を頼る, ～をあてにする ②～による

□ **deposit** 動 ①置く ②預金する ③手付金を払う 名 ①預金, 預かり金 ②手付金

□ **deprive ~ of ...** ～から…を奪う

□ **deprived** 動 deprive(奪う)の過去, 過去分詞 形 恵まれない, 困窮している

□ **depth** 名 深さ, 奥行き, 深いところ

□ **derision** 名 嘲り, 物笑いの種, 愚弄

□ **descent** 名 下り坂, 下降

□ **describe** 動 (言葉で)描写する, 特色を述べる, 説明する

□ **deserve** 動 (～を)受けるに足る, 値する, (～して)当然である

□ **desire** 動 強く望む, 欲する 名 欲望, 欲求, 願望

□ **desolate** 形 荒廃した, 住む人のいない

□ **despite** 前 ～にもかかわらず

□ **detail** 名 ①細部, 《-s》詳細 ②《-s》個人情報 動 詳しく述べる

□ **deteriorate** 動 ①悪化[低下・退廃]する ②悪化させる

□ **determine** 動 ①決心する[させる] ②決定する[させる] ③測定する

□ **devoid** 形 欠けている, 欠いている

□ **diameter** 名 直径

□ **die of** ～がもとで死ぬ

□ **different from** 《be –》～と違う

□ **dilapidated** 形 荒れ果てた, 壊れかけた

□ **diminish** 動 減らす, 減少する, 小さくする

□ **direct** 形 まっすぐな, 直接の, 率直な, 露骨な 副 まっすぐに, 直接に 動 ①指導する, 監督する ②(目・注意・努力などを)向ける

□ **direction** 名 ①方向, 方角 ②《-s》指示, 説明書 ③指導, 指揮

□ **disappear** 動 見えなくなる, 姿を消す, なくなる

□ **disappointed** 動 disappoint(失望させる)の過去, 過去分詞 形 がっかりした, 失望した

□ **disappointment** 名 失望

□ **disclose** 動 (秘密などを)公表する, 暴露する

□ **disharmony** 名 ①〔意見の相違などの〕不調和 ②不協和音

□ **dismissal** 名 ①解放, 放免, 解雇 ②(告訴などの)却下

□ **dismount** 動〔馬・自転車・バイクなどから〕降りる

□ **disoriented** 形 頭が混乱している, うろたえて, しどろもどろの

□ **disown** 動 ①〔～に〕責任[関係]がないと言う ②〔子どもを〕勘当する ③〔～と〕縁を切る

□ **display** 動 展示する, 示す 名 展示, 陳列, 表出

□ **distance** 名 距離, 隔たり, 遠方

□ **distant** 形 ①遠い, 隔たった ②よそよそしい, 距離のある

□ **divide** 動 分かれる, 分ける, 割れる, 割る

□ **divorce** 動 離婚する 名 離婚, 分離

□ **dizzily** 副 ①目まいがして[を覚えながら] ②〔頭が〕クラクラして

□ **do one's best** 全力を尽くす

□ **document** 名 文書, 記録 動 (～を)記録する

□ **doing** 動 do（～をする）の現在分詞 **finish doing** ～するのを終える **stop doing** ～するのをやめる 名 ①すること，したこと ②《-s》行為，出来事

□ **done** 熟 **could have done** ～だったかもしれない《仮定法》

□ **donning** 動 don（身に着ける）の現在分詞

□ **doubt** 名 ①疑い，不確かなこと ②未解決点，困難 動 疑う

□ **down** 熟 **come down** 下りて来る **come down to** ～に伝わる，～に及ぶ **look down on** ～を見下す **run down** 駆け下りる

□ **downright** 形 まったくの，まぎれもない，率直な 副 まったく，すっかり

□ **downward** 形 下方の，下向きの，下降する，以後の 副 下方へ，下向きに，堕落して，～以後

□ **dozen** 名 1ダース，12（個）

□ **drama** 名 劇，演劇，ドラマ，劇的な事件

□ **draw** 動 ①引く，引っ張る ②描く ③引き分けになる［する］

□ **drawn** 動 draw（引く）の過去分詞

□ **dreadfully** 副 恐ろしく，非常に，極度に

□ **dream of** ～を夢見る

□ **drew** 動 draw（引く）の過去

□ **dried** 動 dry（乾燥する）の過去，過去分詞 形 乾燥した

□ **drinking** 動 drink（飲む）の現在分詞 名 飲むこと，飲酒

□ **driven** 動 drive（車で行く）の過去分詞

□ **droopy** 形 ①垂れ下がった，たるんだ ②気持ちが沈んだ，しょげかえった，意気消沈した

□ **droplet** 名 小滴，飛沫

□ **dropping** 名 ①落下（物），降下（物） ②滴，水滴 ③〔動物が落とした〕ふん

□ **due** 形 予定された，期日のきている，支払われるべき **due to** ～によって，～が原因で 名 当然の権利

□ **dull** 形 退屈な，鈍い，くすんだ，ぼんやりした 動 鈍くなる［する］

□ **dumbfounded** 形 あぜんとした，びっくりした

□ **dusk** 名 夕闇，薄暗がり 形 暮れかかった，薄暗い

□ **dusky** 形 ①薄暗い，ほの暗い ②〔色が〕くすんだ

□ **dwelling** 動 dwell（住む）の現在分詞 名 住居，居住

E

□ **earthen** 形 土で作った，土の，陶製の

□ **earthquake** 名 地震，大変動

□ **ease** 名 安心，気楽 動 安心させる，楽にする，ゆるめる

□ **easily** 副 ①容易に，たやすく，苦もなく ②気楽に

□ **easygoing** 形 あくせくしない，のんびりした

□ **eater** 名 食べる人

□ **eaves** 名 ひさし，軒

□ **Echizen** 名 越前《地名》

□ **echo** 名 こだま，反響 動 反響させる［する］

□ **edge** 名 ①刃 ②端，縁 動 ①刃をつける，鋭くする ②縁どる，縁に沿って進む

□ **effect** 名 ①影響，効果，結果 ②実施，発効 動 もたらす，達成する

□ **either A or B** Aかそれとも B

□ **elder** 形 年上の，年長の

□ **elderly** 形 かなり年配の，初老の 名《the –》お年寄り

□ **elegant** 形 上品な，優雅な

□ **else** 熟 **no one else** 他の誰一人として～しない

□ **emaciated** 形〔人が〕痩せ衰えた［こけた］，衰弱した

□ **emboss** 動〔図柄・文字などを〕浮き彫りにする，浮き出させる

□ **emerge** 動 現れる，浮かび上がる，明らかになる

□ **emerged** 動 emerge（現れる，身を起こす）の過去形

□ **emit** 動 ①（におい・光などを）放つ，放出する ②発行する

□ **emotion** 名 感激，感動，感情

□ **emperor** 名 皇帝，天皇

□ **employ** 動 ①（人を）雇う，使う ②利用する 名 雇用，職業

□ **employment** 名 ①雇用 ②仕事，職

□ **empress** 名 女帝，皇后，女王

□ **enable** 動（～することを）可能にする，容易にする

□ **encompass** 動 ①〔～の回りを〕取り囲む，包囲する ②〔～を〕包む，覆う ③〔完全に～を〕包含する，網羅する

□ **encounter** 動（思いがけなく）出会う，遭う 名 遭遇，（思いがけない）出会い

□ **encourage** 動 ①勇気づける ②促進する，助長する

□ **end** 熟 **in the end** とうとう，結局，ついに

□ **endless** 形 終わりのない，無限の

□ **energetic** 形 エネルギッシュな，精力的な，活動的な

□ **energetically** 副 精力的に，力強く，エネルギッシュに

□ **engaged** 動 engage（約束する）の過去，過去分詞 形 ①婚約した ②忙しい，ふさがっている

□ **enough** 熟 **enough to do** ～するのに十分な **more than enough** 十二分に，あり余るくらいに

□ **ensuing** 形 その後に続く［続いて起こった］

□ **entangle** 動（面倒なことに）巻き込む，もつれさせる

□ **entire** 形 全体の，完全な，まったくの

□ **entirely** 副 完全に，まったく

□ **envelope** 名 封筒，包み

□ **equal** 形 等しい，均等な，平等な 動 匹敵する，等しい 名 同等のもの［人］

□ **equivalent** 形 ①同等の，等しい ②同意義の 名 同等のもの，等価なもの

□ **era** 名 時代，年代

□ **establish** 動 確立する，立証する，設置［設立］する

□ **estate** 名 不動産，財産，遺産，地所，土地

□ **eternal** 形 永遠の，永久の

□ **eve** 名 前日，前夜

□ **even if** たとえ～でも

□ **even then** その時でさえ

□ **even though** ～であるけれども，～にもかかわらず

□ **eventually** 副 結局は

□ **ever** 熟 **as ～ as ever** 相変わらず，これまでのように **ever more** これまで以上に

□ **everyone** 代 誰でも，皆

□ **everything** 代 すべてのこと［もの］，何でも，何もかも **everything in the world** この世にある全ての物

□ **evil** 形 ①邪悪な ②有害な，不吉な 名 ①邪悪 ②害，わざわい，不幸 副 悪く

□ **exaggeration** 名 誇張，大げさな表現

□ **examine** 動 試験する，調査［検査］する，診察する

□ **exceptional** 形 例外的な，特別に優れた

☐ **excused** 動《be –》遠慮させてもらう

☐ **exercise** 名 ①運動, 体操 ②練習 動 ①運動する, 練習する ②影響を及ぼす

☐ **exhausted** 動 exhaust（ひどく疲れさせる）の過去, 過去分詞 形 疲れ切った, 消耗した

☐ **existence** 名 存在, 実在, 生存

☐ **expect** 動 予期［予測］する,（当然のこととして）期待する

☐ **explanation** 名 ①説明, 解説, 釈明 ②解釈, 意味

☐ **explicitly** 副〔説明などが〕はっきりと, 明確に

☐ **express** 動 表現する, 述べる

☐ **expression** 名 ①表現, 表示, 表情 ②言い回し, 語句

☐ **extraordinarily** 副 異常に, 並はずれて, 法外に

☐ **extraordinary** 形 異常な, 並はずれた, 驚くべき

☐ **extremely** 副 非常に, 極度に

☐ **extricate** 動〔もつれている状態から〕解放する, 自由にする,〔困難な状況から〕救い出す

☐ **eyelid** 名 まぶた

F

☐ **face to face** 面と向かって

☐ **facial** 形 顔の, 顔に用いる

☐ **fact** 熟 **in fact** つまり, 実は, 要するに

☐ **faded** 形 ①〔光・音などが〕消えかかった, 弱まった ②色あせた

☐ **fail** 動 ①失敗する, 落第する［させる］②《– to ～》～し損なう, ～できない ③失望させる 名 失敗, 落第点

☐ **faintly** 副 かすかに, ぼんやりと, ほのかに, 力なく

☐ **fair** 形 正しい, 公平［正当］な

☐ **fall behind** 取り残される, 後れを取る

☐ **fall on** ～に降りかかる

☐ **fallen** 動 fall（落ちる）の過去分詞 形 落ちた, 倒れた

☐ **famine** 名 飢え, 飢饉, 凶作

☐ **far** 熟 **as far as** ～と同じくらい遠く, ～まで, ～する限り（では） **far from** ～から遠い, ～どころか

☐ **far-off** 形 はるかかなたの

☐ **fastener** 名 締め具, 留め具, ファスナー

☐ **father-in-law** 名 義理の父, 継父, しゅうと

☐ **fawning** 形 へつらう

☐ **fear** 名 ①恐れ ②心配, 不安 動 ①恐れる ②心配する

☐ **feast** 名 ①饗宴, ごちそう ②（宗教上の）祝祭日 ③大きな楽しみ 動 ごちそうになる, もてなす

☐ **feat** 名 偉業, 離れわざ

☐ **feature** 名 ①特徴, 特色 ②顔の一部,《-s》顔立ち

☐ **feeling** 動 feel（感じる）の現在分詞 名 ①感じ, 気持ち ②触感, 知覚 ③同情, 思いやり, 感受性

☐ **feet** 熟 **to one's feet** 両足で立っている状態に

☐ **fellow** 名 ①仲間, 同僚 ②人, やつ 形 仲間の, 同士の

☐ **fervent** 形 熱心な, 熱烈な

☐ **Fifth Ranker**《the –》五位《宮中における位階のひとつ。また, その位の者》

☐ **figure** 名 ①人［物］の姿, 形 ②図（形） ③数字 動 ①描写する, 想像する ②計算する ③目立つ,（～として）現れる

☐ **filled with**《be –》～でいっぱいになる

☐ **finish doing** ～するのを終える

A B C D E F G H I J K L M N O P Q R S T U V W X Y Z

□ **finished** 動 finish (終わる) の過去, 過去分詞 形 ①終わった, 仕上がった ②洗練された ③もうだめになった

□ **finishing** 動 finish (終わる) の現在分詞 形 仕上げの, 最後の 名 仕上げ

□ **firewood** 名 まき, たき木

□ **first** 熟 **at first** 最初は, 初めのうちは **first of all** まず第一に **for the first time** 初めて

□ **fit** 形 適当な, 相応な 動 合致[適合]する, 合致させる

□ **fitting** 名《-s》家具類, 設備

□ **fix** 動 ①固定する[させる] ②修理する ③決定する ④用意する, 整える **fix on** ～にくぎ付けになる

□ **fixedly** 副 固定して, じっと

□ **flake** 名 一片, 薄片

□ **flame** 名 炎, (炎のような) 輝き 動 燃え上がる, (顔などが) さっと赤らむ

□ **flap** 動 はためく, はためかせる

□ **flask** 名〔飲料などを入れる〕筒, フラスコ瓶

□ **flattery** 名 へつらい, お世辞, おべっか

□ **flaw** 名 欠陥, 欠点, ひび 動 損なう

□ **flock** 名 (羊・鳥などの) 群れ, 群集 動 集まる, 群がる

□ **flood** 名 ①洪水 ②殺到 動 ①氾濫する, 氾濫させる ②殺到する

□ **floorboard** 名 床板

□ **floss** 名 真綿, 繭綿, 〔種子の〕綿毛

□ **flow** 動 流れ出る, 流れる, あふれる 名 ①流出 ②流ちょう (なこと)

□ **flush** 動 顔が赤くなる, 赤くなる, ほてる 名 紅潮, 顔が赤くなること

□ **focus** 名 ①焦点, ピント ②関心の的, 着眼点 ③中心 動 ①焦点を合わせる ②(関心・注意を) 集中させる

□ **following** 動 follow (ついていく) の現在分詞 形《the –》次の, 次に続く 名《the –》下記のもの, 以下に述べるもの

□ **foolish** 形 おろかな, ばかばかしい

□ **foolishness** 名 おろかさ, 愚行

□ **foot** 熟 **on foot** 歩いて

□ **footstep** 名 足音, 歩み

□ **for a moment** 熟 少しの間

□ **for a while** しばらくの間, 少しの間

□ **for long** 長い間

□ **for nothing** むだに

□ **for some time** しばらくの間

□ **for some time now** これまでかなりの期間

□ **for the first time** 初めて

□ **for ~ years** ～年間, ～年にわたって

□ **force** 名 力, 勢い 動 ①強制する, 力ずくで～する, 余儀なく～させる ②押しやる, 押し込む

□ **forehead** 名 ひたい

□ **forget to do** ～することを忘れる

□ **forlornly** 副 ①〔人が〕孤独で寂しそうに ②〔物が〕ポツンと取り残されたように ③〔望みなどが〕はかなく, 見込みなく

□ **form** 名 ①形, 形式 ②書式 **take form** (物事が) 形をとる, 具体化する 動 形づくる

□ **formal** 形 正式の, 公式の, 形式的な, 格式ばった

□ **fortunately** 副 幸運にも

□ **forward** 形 ①前方の, 前方へ向かう ②将来の ③先の 副 ①前方に ②将来に向けて ③先へ, 進んで **look forward to** ～を期待する 動 ①転送する ②進める

□ **fox** 名 キツネ (狐)

□ **freedom** 名 ①自由 ②束縛がないこと

□ **freely** 副 自由に, 障害なしに

□ **freeze** 動 ①凍る，凍らせる ②ぞっとする［させる］

□ **friendly** 形 親しみのある，親切な，友情のこもった 副 友好的に，親切に

□ **frigid** 形 きわめて寒い，極寒の

□ **from ~ to ...** ～から…まで

□ **front** 熟 **in front of** ～の前に，～の正面に

□ **frost** 名 霜，寒気，凍結

□ **frost-bitten** 形 霜枯れの，凍傷にかかった

□ **frost-covered** 形 霜に覆われた

□ **frost-filled** 形 霜を含んだ，霜が充満した

□ **frown** 動 しかめ面をする，まゆを寄せる 名 むずかしい顔つき，しかめ面，まゆを寄せること

□ **Fujiwara no Arihito** 藤原有仁《人名，藤原利仁の義父》

□ **Fujiwara no Mototsune** 藤原基経《人名，五位が仕える摂政》

□ **Fujiwara no Tokinaga** 藤原時長《人名，藤原利仁の父で民部卿》

□ **Fujiwara no Toshihito** 藤原利仁《人名，藤原時長の子で基経の恪勤》

□ **fulfill** 動（義務・約束を）果たす，（要求・条件を）満たす

□ **fully** 副 十分に，完全に，まるまる

□ **fun** 熟 **make fun of** ～を物笑いの種にする，からかう

□ **funa** 名《魚》フナ

□ **fur** 名 毛，毛皮（製品）

□ **further** 形 いっそう遠い，その上の，なおいっそうの **further on** これより先，もっと先で 副 いっそう遠く，その上に，もっと 動 促進する

□ **futo** 名 伏菟（ふと）《唐菓子のひとつで，こねた小麦粉を油で焼いた・揚げたもの》

G

□ **gain** 動 ①得る，増す ②進歩する，進む 名 ①増加，進歩 ②利益，得ること，獲得

□ **gait** 名 ①歩き方，足取り ②馬の歩き方 ③進み方，進度

□ **Gankyo** 名《– era》元慶（がんきょう）《日本の元号のひとつで，貞観の後・仁和の前。877–885》

□ **gap** 名 ギャップ，隔たり，すき間 動 すき間ができる

□ **gaping** 形〔亀裂や傷口など〕大きく［ぽっかりと］割れた［口を開けた］

□ **gargantuan** 形 巨大な，途方もない

□ **garment** 名 衣服，《-s》衣料

□ **gasp** 動 ①あえぐ ②はっと息をのむ ③息が止まる 名 ①あえぎ ②息切れ ③息をのむこと

□ **gather** 動 ①集まる，集める ②生じる，増す ③推測する

□ **gathering** 動 gather（集まる）の現在分詞 名 ①集まり，集会 ②ひだ，ギャザー

□ **gaze** 名 凝視，注視 動 凝視する

□ **gecko** 名《動物》ヤモリ

□ **gentle** 形 ①優しい，温和な ②柔らかな

□ **get angry** 腹を立てる

□ **get stuck in** ～にはまり込む

□ **getaway** 名 逃走，逃亡 形 逃走（用）の

□ **gist** 名〔話・説明などの〕主旨，要点

□ **give up** あきらめる，やめる

□ **glee** 名 喜び，歓喜

□ **gloomy** 形 ①憂うつな，陰気な ②うす暗い

□ **go in** 中に入る，開始する

□ **go out of one's way to** わざわざ～する，～するために尽力する

□ **go through** 通り抜ける

☐ **go up** ～に上がる，登る

☐ **goggle** 動〔目玉を〕ぎょろつかせる，目をむく

☐ **gold** 名金，金貨，金製品，金色 形金の，金製の，金色の

☐ **good deal of** 多量の，豊富な

☐ **goodness** 名①善良さ，よいところ ②優秀 ③神《婉曲表現》

☐ **gorge** 名①峡谷，山峡 ②腹いっぱいの食事

☐ **gotten** 動get（得る）の過去分詞

☐ **grab** 動①ふいにつかむ，ひったくる ②横取りする 名ひっつかむこと，横取り

☐ **gradual** 形徐々の，ゆるやかな

☐ **gradually** 副だんだんと

☐ **grapevine** 名《植物》ブドウの木［つる］

☐ **grasp** 動つかむ，握る，とらえる，理解する 名把握，理解（力）

☐ **grass** 名草，牧草（地），芝生 動草［芝生］で覆う［覆われる］

☐ **grave** 名墓 形重要な，厳粛な，落ち着いた

☐ **gravelly** 形①砂利の（ような），砂利混じりの ②〔声が〕ガラガラの，しわがれた，しゃがれた

☐ **gray-hair** 名白髪頭（の）

☐ **gray-haired** 形白髪頭の，白髪交じりの

☐ **grayness** 名灰色であること，灰色の程度

☐ **grilled** 形網焼きにした，焼き網で焼いた

☐ **grin** 動歯を見せて笑う，歯をむき出す 名歯を見せて笑うこと

☐ **groan** 動①うめく，うなる ②ぶうぶう言う 名うめき声

☐ **groom** 名花婿，新郎 動きれいに整える，手入れをする

☐ **growing** 動grow（成長する）の現在分詞 形成長期にある，大きくなりつつある

☐ **growth** 名成長，発展 形成長している

☐ **gruel** 名薄い粥

☐ **guard** 名①警戒，見張り ②番人 動番をする，監視する，守る

☐ **Guardhouse** 名侍所《貴人の傍に控え，その身辺を警護する従者の詰所》

☐ **guest** 名客，ゲスト

H

☐ **hag** 名くそばばあ

☐ **half-remember** 形うろ覚えの，ぼんやりと覚えている

☐ **halfway** 副中間［中途］で，不完全に 形中間［中途］の，不完全な

☐ **hall** 名公会堂，ホール，大広間，玄関

☐ **halt** 動①止まる，停止する ②もたもたする，筋が通らない 名中止，休止

☐ **hand** 熟 **on the other hand** 一方，他方では

☐ **handsome** 形端正な（顔立ちの），りっぱな，（男性が）ハンサムな

☐ **hang** 動かかる，かける，つるす，ぶら下がる 名①かかり具合 ②《the –》扱い方，こつ

☐ **happen to** たまたま～する，～に起こる

☐ **hard to** ～し難い

☐ **hardly** 副①ほとんど～でない，わずかに ②厳しく，かろうじて

☐ **hate** 動嫌う，憎む，（～するのを）いやがる 名憎しみ

☐ **hatred** 名憎しみ，毛嫌い

☐ **haughtily** 副傲慢に，横柄に

☐ **have** 熟 **could have done** ～だったかもしれない《仮定法》 **have no choice but to** ～するしかない

□ **haze** 名かすみ，もや

□ **headgear** 名〔帽子やヘルメットなどの〕かぶり物

□ **headlong** 形①まっさかさまの ②向こう見ずな，軽率な 副①まっさかさまに ②向こう見ずに，軽率に

□ **hearing** 動hear（聞く）の現在分詞 名①聞くこと，聴取，聴力 ②聴聞会，ヒアリング

□ **Heian period** 平安時代《794–1185年頃》

□ **height** 名①高さ，身長 ②《the –》絶頂，真っ盛り ③高台，丘

□ **help** 熟**can't help (but)** ～せずにはいられない **cannot help ～ing** ～せずにはいられない **help oneself to** ～を自分で［自由に］取って食べる［飲む］

□ **hem** 名へり，縁

□ **here and there** あちこちで

□ **hereafter** 副今後は，将来は 名将来，来世

□ **hesitate** 動ためらう，ちゅうちょする

□ **hesitation** 名ためらい，ちゅうちょ

□ **hey** 間①《呼びかけ・注意を促して》おい，ちょっと ②へえ，おや，まあ

□ **hide** 動隠れる，隠す，隠れて見えない，秘密にする

□ **Hiei** 名《Mount –》比叡山

□ **Higashiyama** 名東山《地名》

□ **highwayman** 名追いはぎ

□ **hilt** 名（剣の）つか

□ **hold back** （感情を）抑える，自制する

□ **hold in** （動かないように）押さえる

□ **hold up** （指を）立てる

□ **holding** 動hold（つかむ）の現在分詞 名①握ること ②保持 形保有の

□ **honor** 名①名誉，光栄，信用 ②節操，自尊心 動尊敬する，栄誉を与える

□ **hoof** 名ひづめ

□ **hooves** 名hoof（ひづめ）の複数形

□ **hopeless** 形①希望のない，絶望的な ②勝ち目のない

□ **horizon** 名水平線，地平線

□ **horrible** 形恐ろしい，ひどい

□ **horseback** 名馬の背

□ **how to** ～する方法

□ **however** 副たとえ～でも 接けれども，だが

□ **huge** 形巨大な，ばく大な

□ **human being** 人，人間

□ **humble** 形つつましい，粗末な 動卑しめる，謙虚にさせる

□ **humiliate** 動恥をかかせる，屈辱を与える

□ **hunch** 動（背などを）丸める

□ **hungrily** 副①飢えて，ひもじそうに，物欲しそうに ②渇望して，熱心に

□ **hunting** 動hunt（狩る）の現在分詞 名狩り，狩猟，ハンティング，捜索 形狩猟の

□ **hurriedly** 副大急ぎで，あわてて

□ **hurry on** 急いでする［行く］

□ **husky** 形①ハスキーな［しゃがれた］声の ②〔体格の〕がっちりした，頑丈な

I

□ **icy** 形氷の（多い），氷のように冷たい

□ **identify** 動①（本人・同一と）確認する，見分ける ②意気投合する

□ **if** 熟**as if** あたかも～のように，まるで～みたいに **even if** たとえ～でも **wonder if** ～ではないかと思う

A B C D E F G H I J K L M N O P Q R S T U V W X Y Z

A B C D E F G H I J K L M N O P Q R S T U V W X Y Z

□ **ignore** 動 無視する，怠る
□ **ill-timed** 形 間の悪い，時機を失した
□ **image** 名 ①印象，姿 ②画像，映像 動 心に描く，想像する
□ **imagine** 動 想像する，心に思い描く
□ **imbue** 動〔物に色やにおいなどをしっかり〕染み込ませる
□ **immediately** 副 すぐに，～するやいなや
□ **immense** 形 巨大な，計り知れない，すばらしい
□ **immune** 形 影響を受けない，反応がない
□ **imperial** 形 ①帝国の，皇帝の，皇后の ②荘厳なる
□ **impoverished** 形 ①貧困に陥った，疲弊した ②〔表現などが〕精彩を欠いた，貧弱な
□ **impressive-looking** 形 印象的な見た目をした，見栄えのする
□ **improvise** 動 即興でやる，行き当たりばったりでやる
□ **in addition to** ～に加えて，さらに
□ **in an instant** たちまち，ただちに
□ **in any case** とにかく
□ **in fact** つまり，実は，要するに
□ **in front of** ～の前に，～の正面に
□ **in no way** 決して～でない
□ **in particular** 特に，とりわけ
□ **in piles** 山積みに
□ **in spite of** ～にもかかわらず
□ **in the end** とうとう，結局，ついに
□ **in this way** このようにして
□ **incident** 名 出来事，事故，事変，紛争 形 ①起こりがちな ②付随する
□ **incoherently** 副〔話などが〕矛盾して，支離滅裂に
□ **increasingly** 副 ますます，だんだん
□ **indeed** 副 ①実際，本当に ②《強意》まったく 間 本当に，まさか
□ **indicate** 動 ①指す，示す，(道などを)教える ②それとなく言う ③きざしがある
□ **indifferent** 形 無関心な，無感動な，無頓着な，冷淡な
□ **indigo** 名 藍，藍色 形 藍の，藍色の
□ **indigo-blue** 形 藍青色をした
□ **indistinct** 形 はっきりしない，不明瞭な
□ **individually** 副 個人的に，1つひとつ
□ **inexpert** 形 未熟な，下手な，素人の
□ **inextricable** 形 ①切り離せない，ほどけない ②抜け出せない，解決できない，込み入った
□ **infinitely** 副 無限に
□ **informal** 形 形式ばらない，非公式の
□ **innate** 形 生まれつきの，先天的な，内在的な
□ **inquire** 動 尋ねる，問う
□ **insert** 動 挿入する，入れる，はめ込む 名 挿入(物)
□ **insist** 動 ①主張する，断言する ②要求する
□ **instant** 形 即時の，緊急の，即席の 名 瞬間，寸時 **in an instant** たちまち，ただちに
□ **instantly** 副 すぐに，即座に
□ **instruct** 動 ①教える，教育する ②指図［命令］する
□ **instruction** 名 教えること，指示，助言
□ **insufficient** 形 ①不十分な，不足して ②不適当な，能力のない
□ **intense** 形 ①強烈な，激しい ②感

情的な

□ **intensely** 副 ①〔感情などが〕熱烈に，猛烈に ②〔程度が〕極度に，激しく

□ **intentionally** 副 故意に

□ **interested** 動 interest（興味を起こさせる）の過去，過去分詞 形 興味を持った，関心のある **interested in** 《be –》～に興味［関心］がある

□ **interior** 名 内部，室内，インテリア 形 内部の，室内の，内陸の，国内の

□ **intrigue** 動 ①陰謀を企てる ②好奇心をそそる 名 陰謀（事件）

□ **invisible** 名 目に見えないもの 形 目に見えない，表に出ない

□ **invitation** 名 招待（状），案内（状）

□ **involve** 動 ①含む，伴う ②巻き込む，かかわらせる

□ **issue** 名 ①問題，論点 ②発行物 ③出口，流出 **issue of** ～の問題 動 ①（～から）出る，生じる ②発行する

□ **itch** 名 ①かゆみ ②渇望 動 ①かゆい，むずむずする ②ほしくてたまらない，したくてたまらない

□ **itself** 代 それ自体，それ自身

J

□ **Japanese** 形 日本（人・語）の 名 ①日本人 ②日本語

□ **jaw** 名 ①あご ②《-s》あご状のもの

□ **jester** 名（中世の王侯や貴族に仕えた）道化師

□ **join in** 加わる，参加する

□ **joke** 名 冗談，ジョーク 動 冗談を言う，ふざける，からかう

□ **judge** 動 判決を下す，裁く，判断する，評価する 名 裁判官，判事，審査員

□ **judicial** 形 裁判（官）の，司法の

□ **just as**（ちょうど）であろうとおり

K

□ **Kamogawa** 名《– river》加茂川

□ **Kannon Sutra** 観音経《仏典のひとつ》

□ **keep up** 続ける，（遅れないで）ついていく

□ **kimono** 名 着物

□ **kin** 名 家族，親類

□ **kind of** ～のようなもの［人］

□ **kindness** 名 親切（な行為），優しさ

□ **knee** 名 ひざ

□ **kneel** 動 ひざまずく，ひざをつく

□ **knives** 名 knife（ナイフ）の複数

□ **know nothing of** ～のことを知らない

□ **knowing** 動 know（知っている）の現在分詞 形 物知りの，故意の

□ **Kyoto** 名 京都《地名》

L

□ **lack** 動 不足している，欠けている 名 不足，欠乏

□ **lacquer** 名〔日本の〕漆，漆器，漆細工

□ **ladder** 名 はしご，はしご状のもの

□ **laid** 動 lay（置く）の過去，過去分詞

□ **Lake Biwa** 琵琶湖（= Biwako Lake）

□ **lamp** 名 ランプ，灯火

□ **lantern** 名 手提げランプ，ランタン

□ **lateness** 名 遅いこと，遅れること

□ **latticed** 形 格子造りの

□ **laugh at** ～を見て［聞いて］笑う

□ **laughing** 動 laugh（笑う）の過去分詞 **burst out laughing** 爆笑する 名 笑うこと，笑い（声） 形 笑っている（ような），楽しそうな

□ **laughter** 名 笑い(声)

□ **lay** 動 ①置く, 横たえる, 敷く ②整える ③卵を産む ④lie(横たわる)の過去 **lay out** きちんと並べる, 陳列する

□ **layer** 名 層, 重ね 動 層になる[する]

□ **lead the way** 先に立って導く, 案内する, 率先する

□ **lead to** ～に至る, ～に通じる, ～を引き起こす

□ **lead up to** ～に通じる, ～につながる

□ **leading** 動 lead(導く)の現在分詞 形 主要な, 指導的な, 先頭の

□ **leafless** 形 〔木が〕葉のない, 落葉した

□ **leap** 動 ①跳ぶ ②跳び越える 名 跳ぶこと

□ **least** 形 いちばん小さい, 最も少ない 副 いちばん小さく, 最も少なく 名 最小, 最少 **at least** 少なくとも

□ **leave for** ～に向かって出発する

□ **leave over** 残しておく

□ **leftover** 形 食べ残しの, 残りの 名《-s》食べ残し, 残飯

□ **leisurely** 形 のんびりした, くつろいだ 副 のんびりと, くつろいで

□ **length** 名 長さ, 縦, たけ, 距離

□ **lent** 動 lend(貸す)の過去, 過去分詞

□ **less** 形 ～より小さい[少ない] 副 ～より少なく, ～ほどでなく

□ **lesser** 形 小さいほうの, 劣ったほうの 副 より少なく

□ **let out** (声を)出す, 発する

□ **let slip** (秘密などを)うっかりもらす

□ **letup** 名〈話〉停止, 中止, 〔雨などが〕やむこと

□ **level** 名 ①水平, 平面 ②水準 形 ①水平の, 平たい ②同等[同位]の 動 ①水平にする ②平等にする

□ **lice** 名 louse(シラミ)の複数

□ **lickety-split** 副〈米話〉全速力で

□ **lift** 動 ①持ち上げる, 上がる ②取り除く, 撤廃する

□ **like** 熟 **like this** このような, こんなふうに **look like** ～のように見える, ～に似ている **would like to** ～したいと思う

□ **likely** 形 ①ありそうな, (～)しそうな ②適当な 副 たぶん, おそらく

□ **liking** 動 like(好む)の現在分詞 名 好み, 趣味

□ **linger** 動 長居する, 後まで残る, ぐずぐずする

□ **lingering** 形 長びく, なごり惜しそうな, なかなか消えない

□ **lip** 名 唇, 《-s》口

□ **list** 名 名簿, 目録, 一覧表 動 名簿[目録]に記入する

□ **lit** 動 light(火をつける)の過去, 過去分詞

□ **liter** 名 リットル, リッター

□ **little need to do** ～する必要などほとんどない

□ **living** 動 live(住む)の現在分詞 名 生計, 生活 形 ①生きている, 現存の ②使用されている ③そっくりの

□ **logically** 副 論理的に

□ **loglike** 形 丸太のような

□ **long** 熟 **for long** 長い間 **long ago** ずっと前に, 昔 **no longer** もはや～でない[～しない]

□ **long-ago** 形 ずっと昔[以前]の, 遠い昔の

□ **long-held** 形 かねての, 長年抱いてきた

□ **longingly** 副 切望して, 物欲しげに〔～を見る〕

□ **look back at** ～に視線を戻す, ～を振り返って見る

□ **look down on** ～を見下す

□ **look forward to** ～を期待する

□ **look like** ～のように見える，～に似ている

□ **look over** ～越しに見る，～を見渡す

□ **look to** ～しようとする

□ **look up** 見上げる

□ **look up at** ～の方に顔を上げる

□ **lord** 名 首長，主人，領主，貴族，上院議員

□ **lose sight of** ～を見失う

□ **loss** 名 ①損失（額・物），損害，浪費 ②失敗，敗北 **at a loss** 途方に暮れて

□ **loudly** 副 大声で，騒がしく

□ **low-ranking** 形 下級の，地位の低い

□ **lower** 形 もっと低い，下級の，劣った 動 下げる，低くする

□ **lowering** 形 ①低下させる ②陰鬱な，不機嫌な ③〔空模様が〕険悪な，今にも雨が降りそうな

□ **lull** 名 ①一時的な休止［静けさ］，小やみ ②気持ちを和らげる［静める］もの，落ち着いた状態

□ **lustrous** 形 ①光沢のある ②〔経歴などが〕輝かしい

□ **luxurious** 形 ぜいたくな，豪華な，最高級の

□ **lying** 動 lie（うそをつく・横たわる）の現在分詞

M

□ **maidservant** 名〈古〉〔大きな屋敷の〕お手伝い，召使い

□ **main** 形 主な，主要な

□ **maintain** 動 ①維持する ②養う

□ **make fun of** ～を物笑いの種にする，からかう

□ **make one's way to** ～に向かって進む

□ **make up** 作り出す，～を構成［形成］する

□ **make use of** ～を利用する，～を生かす

□ **making** 動 make（作る）の現在分詞 名 制作，製造

□ **maliciousness** 名 悪意のあること，意地の悪さ

□ **manage** 動 ①動かす，うまく処理する ②経営［管理］する，支配する ③どうにか～する

□ **manly** 形 ①男らしい，断固とした ②男のような

□ **manner** 名 ①方法，やり方 ②態度，様子 ③《-s》行儀，作法，生活様式

□ **mansion** 名 大邸宅

□ **marriage** 名 ①結婚（生活・式）②結合，融合，（吸収）合併

□ **marry** 動 結婚する

□ **mat** 名 マット，敷物

□ **matter** 熟 **matter of**《a－》およそ～，わずか～ **no matter what** たとえどんな～であろうと

□ **meager** 形 やせた，貧弱な

□ **mean-spirited** 形 ①卑劣な，意地悪な ②心の狭い，狭量な

□ **meaning** 名 ①意味，趣旨 ②重要性

□ **meaningfully** 副 意味があるように

□ **meaningless** 形 無意味な，つまらない

□ **meanness** 名 ①貧弱さ，粗悪，つまらなさ ②けち，吝嗇

□ **meanwhile** 副 それまでの間，一方では

□ **meeting** 動 meet（会う）の現在分詞 名 ①集まり，ミーティング，面会 ②競技会

□ **mellow** 形 熟した，芳醇な 動 熟させる，熟す

□ **mention** 動（～について）述べる，言及する 名 言及，陳述

□ **mere** 形 単なる，ほんの，まったく～にすぎない

□ **merge** 動 合併する［させる］，融合する［させる］，溶け込む［ませる］

□ **merrymaker** 名 浮かれ騒ぐ人

□ **messenger** 名 使者，（伝言・小包などの）配達人，伝達者

□ **meter** 名 ①メートル《長さの単位》②計量器，計量する人

□ **midst** 名 真ん中，中央

□ **midway** 副 中途に，中ほどに

□ **might** 助《mayの過去》①～かもしれない ②～してもよい，～できる 名 力，権力

□ **Miidera** 名《– temple》三井寺

□ **military** 形 軍隊［軍人］の，軍事の 名《the –》軍，軍部

□ **mince** 動 細かく刻む 名 ひき肉

□ **mind** 名 ①心，精神，考え ②知性 動 ①気にする，いやがる ②気をつける，用心する

□ **minister** 名 ①大臣，閣僚，公使 ②聖職者

□ **mirror** 名 鏡 動 映す

□ **miserable** 形 みじめな，哀れな

□ **misleading** 動 mislead（間違った方向へ導く）の現在分詞 形 人を誤らせる，誤解を招くような

□ **mist** 名 ①霧，もや，蒸気 ②（目の）かすみ 動 ①霧がかかる，霧で覆う ②（目が）かすむ

□ **mixture** 名 ①混合 ②入り混じったもの

□ **mock** 動 ①あざける，まねをしてからかう ②だます，無効にする 形 うわべの，まがいの，模擬の

□ **mockery** 名 あざけり，冷やかし，笑いもの

□ **mocking** 形 あざける（ような）

□ **mockingly** 副 あざけるように，からかって

□ **modern** 形 現代［近代］の，現代的な，最近の 名 現代［近代］人

□ **modest** 形 控えめな，謙虚な

□ **modesty** 名 謙遜，謙虚さ，つつましさ，しとやかさ

□ **moment** 名 ①瞬間，ちょっとの間 ②（特定の）時，時期 **at the moment** 今は **for a moment** 少しの間

□ **monk** 名 修道士，僧

□ **monkey** 名 サル（猿） 動 ふざける，いたずらをする

□ **monkey-like** 形 サルのような

□ **mood** 名 気分，機嫌，雰囲気，憂うつ

□ **more** 熟 **ever more** これまで以上に **more than** ～以上 **more than enough** 十二分に，あり余るくらいに **no more** もう～ない **the more ~ the more …** ～すればするほどますます…

□ **moreover** 副 その上，さらに

□ **mostly** 副 主として，多くは，ほとんど

□ **mother-of-pearl** 形 真珠（質）層の，真珠色の

□ **motionless** 形 動きのない，静止の

□ **mount** 動（山などに）登る，（馬に）乗る，のせる 名 山《ふつうMt.と略して山名に用いる》

□ **Mount Hiei** 比叡山

□ **mouthful** 名 口いっぱい，一口分

□ **moved** 形《be –》感激する，感銘する

□ **movement** 名 ①動き，運動 ②《-s》行動 ③引っ越し ④変動

□ **moving** 動 move（動く）の現在分詞 形 ①動いている ②感動させる

□ **much** 熟 **too much** 過度の

□ **mugwort** 名《植物》ヨモギ

□ **mumble** 動 ぶつぶつ言う，つぶやく

□ **murder** 名 人殺し，殺害，殺人事件

動殺す

☐ **muscle** 名筋肉, 腕力 動強引に押し進む, 力ずくで進む

☐ **mustache** 名《-s》口ひげ

☐ **mutt** 名①〈俗〉雑種犬 ②〈俗〉ばか, 間抜け

☐ **mutter** 動ぶつぶつ文句を言う, つぶやく 名つぶやき

N

☐ **naive** 形世間知らずの, 単純な, うぶな, だまされやすい

☐ **naked** 形①裸の, むき出しの ②覆いのない, ありのままの

☐ **narrow** 形①狭い ②限られた 動狭くなる［する］

☐ **native** 形①出生（地）の, 自国の ②（～に）固有の, 生まれつきの, 天然の 名（ある土地に）生まれた人

☐ **naturalist** 名①自然主義者 ②博物学者

☐ **naturally** 副生まれつき, 自然に, 当然

☐ **nearby** 形近くの, 間近の 副近くで, 間近で

☐ **nearly** 副①近くに, 親しく ②ほとんど, あやうく

☐ **necessity** 名必要, 不可欠, 必要品

☐ **need** 熟 **little need to do** ～する必要などほとんどない **no need to do** ～する必要はない **only need to do** ～すれば十分

☐ **needless** 形不必要な

☐ **negligently** 副過失で, 怠慢で, 無頓着に

☐ **newly** 副再び, 最近, 新たに

☐ **Ninna** 名《－era》仁和（にんな）《日本の元号のひとつで, 元慶の後・寛平の前。885–889》

☐ **no** 熟 **have no choice but to** ～するしかない **in no way** 決して～でない **no longer** もはや～でない［～しない］ **no matter what** たとえどんな～であろうと **no more** もう～ない **no need to do** ～する必要はない **no one** 誰も［一人も］～ない **no one else** 他の誰一人として～しない

☐ **nobility** 名①高貴さ ②《the－》貴族

☐ **nobleman** 名貴族, 高貴の生まれの人

☐ **none** 代（～の）何も［誰も・少しも］…ない

☐ **nostalgically** 副郷愁を抱いて, 懐かしそうに

☐ **not only ~ but (also) ...** ～だけでなく…もまた

☐ **not yet** まだ～してない

☐ **nothing** 熟 **for nothing** むだに **know nothing of** ～のことを知らない **nothing but** ただ～だけ, ～にすぎない

☐ **notice** 名①注意 ②通知 ③公告 動①気づく, 認める ②通告する

☐ **notion** 名観念, 概念, 意志

☐ **now** 熟 **for some time now** これまでかなりの期間 **now and then** ときどき **now that** 今や～だから, ～からには

☐ **number of** 《a－》いくつかの～, 多くの～, 《the－》～の数

☐ **numerous** 形多数の

O

☐ **object** 名①物, 事物 ②目的物, 対象 動反対する, 異議を唱える

☐ **oblige** 動①（～を）余儀なくさせる, しいる ②要望にこたえる ③恩恵を与える, 《受け身形で》感謝している

☐ **obsess** 動支配する, つきまとう, 頭から離れない

☐ **obstruct** 動ふさぐ, 妨害する

A B C D E F G H I J K L M N O P Q R S T U V W X Y Z

□ **occupy** 動 ①占領する，保有する ②居住する ③占める ④（職に）つく，従事する

□ **occur** 動（事が）起こる，生じる，（考えなどが）浮かぶ

□ **octopus** 名 タコ《軟体動物》

□ **of course** もちろん，当然

□ **offer** 動 申し出る，申し込む，提供する 名 提案，提供

□ **oil** 名 ①油，石油 ②油絵の具，油絵 動 油を塗る［引く］，滑らかにする

□ **Omi** 名 近江（おうみ）《地名》

□ **on and on** 延々と，長々と，引き続き

□ **on foot** 歩いて

□ **on one's own** 自力で

□ **on one's way** 出て行く，出掛ける

□ **on the other hand** 一方，他方では

□ **on the surface of** ～の表面に

□ **one day**（過去の）ある日，（未来の）いつか

□ **one of** ～の1つ［人］

□ **one of these days** いずれそのうちに，近いうちに，近日中に

□ **one side of** ～の片側

□ **one-third** 名 3分の1

□ **oneself** 熟 **help oneself to** ～を自分で［自由に］取って食べる［飲む］

□ **only** 熟 **not only ～ but (also) …** ～だけでなく…もまた **only need to do** ～すれば十分

□ **onto** 前 ～の上へ［に］

□ **opposite** 形 反対の，向こう側の 前 ～の向こう側に 名 反対の人［物］

□ **ordinarily** 副 ①通常は ②普通に，人並みに

□ **original** 形 ①始めの，元の，本来の ②独創的な 名 原型，原文

□ **other** 熟 **on the other hand** 一方，他方では

□ **otherwise** 副 さもないと，そうでなければ

□ **out of** ～から外へ，～から作り出して，～から離れて

□ **outcome** 名 結果，結末

□ **outsider** 名 よそ者，部外者，門外漢

□ **outstretched** 形〔両腕・指などが〕いっぱいに伸ばされた

□ **over there** あそこに

□ **overflowing** 形〔容器に入った液体などが〕あふれそうな，あふれんばかりの

□ **overslept** 動 oversleep（寝過ごす）の過去，過去分詞

□ **overwhelming** 動 overwhelm（力で圧倒する）の現在分詞 形 圧倒的な，圧勝の

□ **own** 熟 **on one's own** 自力で

□ **ox** 名 雄牛

□ **oxen** 名 ox（雄牛）の複数形

P

□ **paid** 動 pay（払う）の過去，過去分詞 形 有給の，支払い済みのの

□ **pair** 名（2つから成る）一対，一組，ペア 動 対になる［する］

□ **palace** 名 宮殿，大邸宅

□ **pale** 形 ①（顔色・人が）青ざめた，青白い ②（色が）薄い，（光が）薄暗い 動 ①青ざめる，青ざめさせる ②淡くなる［する］，色あせる

□ **pall** 名 覆って暗くする物，陰鬱

□ **palm** 名 手のひら（状のもの）

□ **pampas** 名 大草原

□ **panic** 名 パニック，恐慌 動 恐慌を引き起こす，うろたえる

□ **pantless** 形 パンツ［ズボン］をはいてない

□ **parrot** 名オウム 動おうむ返しに言う

□ **part** 熟 **play a part** 役目を果たす

□ **partake** 動〔出されたものを〕食べる, 飲む

□ **particular** 形①特別の ②詳細な **in particular** 特に, とりわけ 名事項, 細部, 《-s》詳細

□ **particularly** 副特に, とりわけ

□ **partner** 名配偶者, 仲間, 同僚 動（～と）組む, 提携する

□ **partook** 動 partake（〔出されたものを〕食べる, 飲む）の過去形

□ **pass by** ～のそばを通る〔通り過ぎる〕

□ **passage** 名①通過, 通行, 通路 ②一節, 経過

□ **passing** 動 pass（過ぎる）の現在分詞 形通り過ぎる, 一時的な 名①通行, 通過 ②合格, 及第

□ **past** 形過去の, この前の 名過去（の出来事） 前《時間・場所》～を過ぎて, ～を越して 副通り越して, 過ぎて

□ **patch** 名継ぎはぎ, 継ぎ, 傷当て 動継ぎを当てる, 一時的に繕う

□ **pathetic** 形哀れな, 感傷的な

□ **patiently** 副我慢強く, 根気よく

□ **peacefully** 副平和に, 穏やかに

□ **peddler** 名行商人

□ **peer** 動じっと見る 名①同等の人, 同僚 ②貴族

□ **perhaps** 副たぶん, ことによると

□ **period** 名①期, 期間, 時代 ②ピリオド, 終わり

□ **persimmon** 名カキ（柿）

□ **personal** 形①個人の, 私的な ②本人自らの

□ **pheasant** 名キジ（雉）《鳥》

□ **pick off** ～をもぎとる

□ **pick up** 拾い上げる

□ **picky** 形〔人が〕えり好みする, 小うるさい, 口やかましい

□ **pierce** 動①突き刺す, 貫く, ～に穴をあける ②身にしみる ③見抜く

□ **pile** 名積み重ね, （～の）山 **in piles** 山積みに 動積み重ねる, 積もる **pile up** 積み重ねる

□ **pillar** 名①柱, 支柱, 支え ②根幹

□ **pillow** 名まくら

□ **pimple** 名吹き出物, にきび, 腫れ物

□ **pine** 名マツ（松）, マツ材

□ **pitch** 名松やに, ピッチ

□ **pitiful** 形①哀れな, 痛々しい ②浅ましい

□ **place** 熟 **take place** 行われる, 起こる

□ **plain** 形①明白な, はっきりした ②簡素な ③平らな ④不細工な, 平凡な 副はっきりと, まったく 名高原, 草原

□ **play a part** 役目を果たす

□ **pleated** 形プリーツの, ひだのある

□ **plod** 動とぼとぼと〔重い足取りで〕歩く

□ **pluck** 動ぐいと引っ張る, 引き抜く, むしる

□ **plume** 名（大きな）羽

□ **pm** 略午後（= post meridiem）

□ **point** 熟 **at this point** 現在のところ **point out** 指し示す, 指摘する **to the point of**〔程度・段階などが〕～まで, ～するまでに, ～ほどに

□ **pointed** 動 point（指す）の過去, 過去分詞 形先のとがった, 鋭い

□ **Police and Judicial Office** 《the –》検非違使（けびいし）《京都の治安維持と民政を所管する役人》

□ **pommel** 名鞍頭

□ **poorly** 副①貧しく, 乏しく ②へたに

□ **pop** 動〔驚きなどで目が〕飛び出す,

A B C D E F G H I J K L M N O **P** Q R S T U V W X Y Z

大きく見開く **pop out** 急に飛び出る

☐ **porridge** 名 かゆ，ポリッジ《穀物を水などで煮たかゆ状のもの》

☐ **porter** 名 ポーター，運搬人，ボーイ

☐ **positively** 副 明確に，確かに，積極的に

☐ **possess** 動 ①持つ，所有する ②(心などを)保つ，制御する

☐ **possessed** 動 possess (持つ)の過去，過去分詞 形 取りつかれた

☐ **possession** 名 ①所有(物) ②財産，領土

☐ **possible** 形 ①可能な ②ありうる，起こりうる **as ～ as possible** できるだけ～

☐ **possibly** 副 ①あるいは，たぶん ②《否定文，疑問文で》どうしても，できる限り，とても，なんとか

☐ **pour** 動 ①注ぐ，浴びせる ②流れ出る，流れ込む ③ざあざあ降る

☐ **practical** 形 ①実際的な，実用的な，役に立つ ②経験を積んだ

☐ **predatory** 形 ①〔動物が〕捕食性の，肉食の ②略奪する，搾取する

☐ **predict** 動 予測[予想]する

☐ **prefer** 動 (～のほうを)好む，(～のほうが)よいと思う

☐ **pressing** 動 press (圧する)の現在分詞 形 差し迫った，緊急の

☐ **prevent** 動 ①妨げる，じゃまする ②予防する，守る，《－ ～ from …》～が…できない[しない]ようにする

☐ **prick** 動 刺す，穴をあける

☐ **pride** 名 誇り，自慢，自尊心 動《－ oneself》誇る，自慢する

☐ **prince** 名 王子，プリンス

☐ **principal** 形 主な，第一の，主要な，重要な

☐ **prior** 形 (時間・順序が)前の，(～に)優先する，(～より)重要な

☐ **probably** 副 たぶん，あるいは

☐ **proceed** 動 進む，進展する，続ける

☐ **process** 名 ①過程，経過，進行 ②手順，方法，製法，加工

☐ **prodigious** 形 巨大の，桁はずれの

☐ **profusely** 副 ①豊富に，豊かに ②過度に，やたらと

☐ **progress** 名 ①進歩，前進 ②成り行き，経過 動 前進する，上達する

☐ **proper** 形 ①適した，適切な，正しい ②固有の

☐ **prospective** 形 期待される，未来の

☐ **protagonist** 名 主人公，指導者，主唱者

☐ **protrude** 動 突き出る，出っ張る

☐ **proudly** 副 ①誇らしげに ②うぬぼれて

☐ **province** 名 ①州，省 ②地方，田舎 ③範囲，領域

☐ **puddle** 名 ①水たまり ②こね土

☐ **pull out** 引き抜く，引き出す

☐ **purple** 形 紫色の 名 紫色

☐ **purposely** 副 わざと，故意に

☐ **pus** 名 膿，膿汁

☐ **pus-filled** 形 膿が詰まった

☐ **push back** 押し返す，押しのける

☐ **putrid** 形 〈動植物が〉腐敗した，悪臭を放つ

Q

☐ **quality** 名 ①質，性質，品質 ②特性 ③良質

☐ **quarter** 名 ①4分の1，25セント，15分，3カ月 ②方面，地域 ③部署 動 4等分する

☐ **quaver** 動〔体・声・音が〕震える

☐ **quickly** 副 敏速に，急いで

☐ **quietly** 副 ①静かに ②平穏に，控

えめに

□ **quip** 名 ①気の利いた[機知に富んだ]言葉, しゃれ ②〔巧みな〕皮肉, からかい

□ **quiver** 動 ぶるぶる震える, 揺れる

R

□ **rabbit** 名 ①ウサギ(兎), ウサギの毛皮 ②弱虫

□ **raise** 動 ①上げる, 高める ②起こす ③〜を育てる ④(資金を)調達する 名 高める[上げる]こと, 昇給

□ **ramble** 動 ぶらぶら歩き回る 名 ぶらぶら歩き

□ **rang** 動 ring (鳴る) の過去

□ **range** 名 列, 連なり, 範囲 動 ①並ぶ, 並べる ②およぶ

□ **rank** 名 ①列 ②階級, 位 動 ①並ぶ, 並べる ②分類する

□ **ranker** 名 ①その地位にいる人 ②並べる人, 整列する[させる]人

□ **rare** 形 ①まれな, 珍しい, 逸品の ②希薄な

□ **rashly** 副 〔行動・判断などが〕軽率に, 早まって

□ **Rashomon** 名 羅生門《朱雀大路にある平安京の正門である羅城門がモデル》

□ **rather** 副 ①むしろ, かえって ②かなり, いくぶん, やや ③それどころか逆に **rather than** 〜よりむしろ

□ **ray** 名 ①光線, 放射線 ②光明

□ **reaction** 名 反応, 反動, 反抗, 影響

□ **reader** 名 ①読者 ②読本, リーダー

□ **readily** 副 ①すぐに, さっそく ②快く, 進んで

□ **reality** 名 現実, 実在, 真実(性)

□ **realization** 名 ①理解, 認識 ②実現

□ **realize** 動 理解する, 実現する

□ **reason for** 〜の理由

□ **reassure** 動 安心させる

□ **recall** 動 思い出す, 思い出させる, 呼び戻す, 回収する 名 呼び戻し, リコール

□ **recite** 動 暗唱する, 復唱する, 物語る, 朗読する

□ **recognize** 動 認める, 認識[承認]する

□ **red-lacquered** 形 丹塗りの

□ **red-nosed** 形 赤鼻の

□ **refill** 動 詰め替える, 補充する

□ **reflect** 動 映る, 反響する, 反射する

□ **refuse** 動 拒絶する, 断る 名 くず, 廃物

□ **regard** 動 ①(〜を…と)見なす ②尊敬する, 重きを置く ③関係がある

□ **regardless** 形 無頓着な, 注意しない 副 それにもかかわらず, それでも

□ **regent** 名 〔君主に代わる〕摂政, 関白, 執権

□ **register** 動 登録する, 署名する, 書留にする 名 一覧表, 記録

□ **regret** 動 後悔する, 残念ながら〜する 名 遺憾, 後悔, (〜に対する)悲しみ

□ **regular** 形 ①規則的な, 秩序のある ②定期的な, 一定の, 習慣的

□ **rein** 名 手綱, 拘束, 統制, 統御力, 支配権, 指揮権 動 手綱で御する, 制御する, 制止する

□ **relentlessly** 副 容赦なく, 冷酷に, 執拗に

□ **relief** 名 (苦痛・心配などの)除去, 軽減, 安心, 気晴らし

□ **religious** 形 ①宗教の ②信心深い

□ **remain** 動 ①残っている, 残る ②(〜の)ままである[いる] 名《-s》①残り(もの) ②遺跡

□ **remaining** 動 remain (残ってい

る）の現在分詞 形残った，残りの

□ **remark** 名①注意，注目，観察 ②意見，記事，批評 動①注目する ②述べる，批評する

□ **remarkable** 形①異常な，例外的な ②注目に値する，すばらしい

□ **remount** 動〔自転車や馬などに〕再びまたがる

□ **remove** 動①取り去る，除去する ②（衣類を）脱ぐ

□ **repair** 動修理［修繕］する 名修理，修繕

□ **repeated** 動 repeat（繰り返す）の過去，過去分詞 形繰り返された，度重なる

□ **repeatedly** 副繰り返して，たびたび

□ **reply** 動答える，返事をする，応答する 名答え，返事，応答

□ **reproach** 動非難する，叱る 名非難，叱責

□ **resemble** 動似ている

□ **residence** 名住宅，居住

□ **resist** 動抵抗［反抗・反撃］する，耐える

□ **resolve** 動決心する，解決する 名決心，決意

□ **resort** 動①手段に訴える ②行く，通う

□ **respect** 名①尊敬，尊重 ②注意，考慮 動尊敬［尊重］する

□ **respectfully** 副うやうやしく，つつしんで，丁重に

□ **response** 名応答，反応，返答

□ **responsibility** 名①責任，義務，義理 ②負担，責務

□ **restless** 形落ち着かない，不安な

□ **result** 名結果，成り行き，成績 動（結果として）起こる，生じる，結局〜になる

□ **resurface** 動①〔沈んだ後で〕再浮上する ②〔いなくなった後で〕再び現れる

□ **retain** 動①保つ，持ち続ける ②覚えている

□ **retired** 動 retire（引き下がる）の過去，過去分詞 形退職した，引退した

□ **return to** 〜に戻る，〜に帰る

□ **reveal** 動明らかにする，暴露する，もらす

□ **revert** 動（前の状態に）戻る，復帰する

□ **ridicule** 動あざ笑う，笑いものにする，からかう 名あざけり，からかい

□ **riding** 動 ride（乗る）の現在分詞 名乗馬，乗車

□ **right** 熟 **all right** 大丈夫で，申し分ない，承知した

□ **ripple** 名さざ波（のような音），波状（の動き），波紋，ざわめき

□ **rising** 形昇る，高まる

□ **riverbed** 名川床，河床

□ **roadside** 名道端，路傍 形道端の

□ **robe** 名①ローブ，化粧着，部屋着 ②《-s》式服，法衣

□ **roll** 動①転がる，転がす ②（波などが）うねる，横揺れする ③（時が）たつ 名①一巻き ②名簿，目録

□ **roof** 名屋根（のようなもの），住居 動屋根をつける

□ **root** 名①根，根元 ②根源，原因 ③《-s》先祖，ルーツ 動根づかせる，根づく

□ **rope** 名綱，なわ，ロープ 動なわで縛る

□ **rub** 動①こする，こすって磨く ②すりむく 名摩擦

□ **rumor** 名うわさ

□ **run down** 駆け下りる

□ **run off** 走り去る，逃げ去る

□ **run through** 走り抜ける

□ **rung** 動 ring（鳴る）の過去分詞

□ **running** 動 run（走る）の現在分詞 名 ランニング，競走 形 ①走っている ②上演中の ③連続する

□ **runny** 形 ①流れやすい ②鼻水［涙］の出る

□ **rush** 動 突進する，せき立てる 名 突進，突撃，殺到

□ **rustic** 形 田舎風の，素朴な，田舎くさい 名 田舎者

S

□ **sacrifice** 動（～に）生け贄をささげる，（～のために）犠牲になる

□ **saddle** 名（自転車などの）サドル，（馬などの）鞍

□ **safely** 副 安全に，間違いなく

□ **sag** 動 たるむ，垂れ下がる，下がる 名 たるみ，垂れ，下落，沈下

□ **Sakamoto** 名 坂本《地名》

□ **sake** 名（～の）ため，利益，目的

□ **sake-loving** 形 酒飲みの

□ **salmon** 名 サケ（鮭），サーモン

□ **same** 熟 **the same ～ as [that] …** …と同じ（ような）～

□ **samurai** 名 侍

□ **sandal** 名《通例-s》サンダル

□ **Sanjobomon** 名 三条坊門《平安京の小路》

□ **sank** 動 sink（沈む）の過去

□ **sash** 名〔腰に付ける幅広の〕帯

□ **sashinuki** 名 指貫（さしぬき）《裾を紐で指し貫いて絞れるようにした袴》

□ **satisfaction** 名 満足

□ **satisfactorily** 副 満足のいくように

□ **satisfy** 動 ①満足させる，納得させる ②（義務を）果たす，償う

□ **saying** 動 say（言う）の現在分詞 名 ことわざ，格言，発言

□ **scarce** 形 ①まれな，珍しい ②少ない

□ **scatter** 動 ①ばらまく，分散する ②《be -ed》散在する

□ **scope** 名 範囲，視野

□ **scramble** 動 ①はい進む，よじ登る ②緊急発進する ③ごちゃごちゃに混ぜる，混乱させる［する］

□ **scrap** 動 ①くずとして捨てる ②（計画などを）やめる

□ **scratch** 動 ひっかく，傷をつける，はがし取る 名 ひっかき傷，かくこと

□ **scrawny** 形 痩せこけた，骨張った，貧相な

□ **scruff** 名 襟首，首筋，うなじ

□ **scrupulous** 形 きちょうめんな，実直な，慎重な

□ **sea bream** タイ科の魚

□ **search** 動 捜し求める，調べる 名 捜査，探索，調査

□ **see ～ as …** ～を…と考える

□ **seem** 動（～に）見える，（～のように）思われる **seem to be** ～であるように思われる

□ **Sekiyama** 名 関山《関所のある山のこと。特に，逢坂関のある逢坂山を指すことがある》

□ **sense** 名 ①感覚，感じ ②《-s》意識，正気，本性 ③常識，分別，センス ④意味 動 感じる，気づく

□ **sentimentalism** 名 感情的傾向，感情主義

□ **serenely** 副〔精神的に〕落ち着いて

□ **series** 名 一続き，連続，シリーズ

□ **servant** 名 ①召使，使用人，しもべ ②公務員，（公共事業の）従業員

□ **serve** 動 ①仕える，奉仕する ②（客の）応対をする，給仕する，食事［飲み物］を出す ③（役目を）果たす，務める，役に立つ

□ **set off** 出発する，発射する

☐ **setting** 動 set（置く）の現在分詞 名 設定，周囲の環境

☐ **settle** 動 ①安定する［させる］，落ち着く，落ち着かせる ②《- in ～》～に移り住む，定住する

☐ **shabbiness** 名〔身なりの〕みすぼらしさ

☐ **shabby** 形 みすぼらしい，粗末な，貧相な，卑しい

☐ **shadow** 名 ①影，暗がり ②亡霊 動 ①陰にする，暗くする ②尾行する

☐ **shaggy** 形 ①毛むくじゃらの，むさくるしい ②粗野な，がさつな，価値のない

☐ **shake** 動 ①振る，揺れる，揺さぶる，震える ②動揺させる 名 ①振ること

☐ **Shall I ～?**（私が）～しましょうか。

☐ **sharp** 形 ①鋭い，とがった ②刺すような，きつい ③鋭敏な ④急な 副 ①鋭く，急に ②（時間が）ちょうど

☐ **sheath** 名〔刀剣の〕さや

☐ **sheathe** 動（剣を）さやに納める

☐ **shifted** 動 shift（動く，方向を変える）の過去形

☐ **shine** 動 ①光る，輝く ②光らせる，磨く 名 光，輝き

☐ **Shinsen'en** 名《－garden》神泉苑《平安京大内裏に接して造営された禁苑（天皇のための庭園）》

☐ **shone** 動 shine（光る）の過去，過去分詞

☐ **shook** 動 shake（振る）の過去

☐ **shore** 名 岸，海岸，陸

☐ **shortcoming** 名 欠点，短所，弱点

☐ **shoulder** 名 肩 動 肩にかつぐ，肩で押し分けて進む

☐ **shout out** 大声で叫ぶ

☐ **shown** 動 show（見せる）の過去分詞

☐ **shrimp** 名 小エビ，シュリンプ

☐ **shrubbery** 名 低木（の植え込み）

☐ **shuffle** 動（足を）引きずる **shuffle along** 足を引きずって歩く，すり足で歩く 名 足を引きずって歩くこと

☐ **shutter** 名 シャッター，雨戸，（カメラの）シャッター

☐ **side** 名 側，横，そば，斜面 **by the side of** ～のそばに **one side of** ～の片側 **side by side** 並んで 形 ①側面の，横の ②副次的な 動（～の）側につく，賛成する

☐ **sideburn** 名 もみあげ

☐ **sight** 熟 **lose sight of** ～を見失う

☐ **silence** 名 沈黙，無言，静寂 動 沈黙させる，静める

☐ **silently** 副 静かに，黙って

☐ **silk** 名 絹（布），生糸 形 絹の，絹製の

☐ **silver** 名 銀，銀貨，銀色 形 銀製の

☐ **simply** 副 ①簡単に ②単に，ただ ③まったく，完全に

☐ **simultaneously** 副 同時に，一斉に

☐ **single** 形 ①たった1つの ②1人用の，それぞれの ③独身の ④片道の

☐ **sire** 名 主君，殿《王・支配者などへの呼び掛け》

☐ **sit on** ～の上に乗る

☐ **situation** 名 ①場所，位置 ②状況，境遇，立場

☐ **skewer** 名 串，焼き串

☐ **slant** 動 傾く，傾ける，傾斜する

☐ **slanting** 形 傾いた

☐ **slap** 動（平手，平たいもので）ぴしゃりと打つ 名 ①平手打ち ②スラッシュ，斜線記号

☐ **sleepy** 形 ①眠い，眠そうな ②活気のない

☐ **sleeve** 名 袖，たもと，スリーブ

☐ **slice** 名 薄切りの1枚，部分 動 薄く切る

□ **slight** 形 ①わずかな ②ほっそりして ③とるに足らない

□ **slip** 動 滑る，滑らせる，滑って転ぶ **let slip**（秘密などを）うっかりもらす 名 滑ること

□ **slope** 動 傾斜する［させる］，坂になる，勾配をつける 名 坂，斜面，傾斜

□ **sloping** 形 傾斜した

□ **sloppy** 形 ①泥んこの，びしょびしょの ②雑な，だらしのない，いい加減な ③感傷的な，めそめそした

□ **slowly** 副 遅く，ゆっくり

□ **smiling** 形 微笑する，にこにこした

□ **smoke** 動 喫煙する，煙を出す 名 煙，煙状のもの

□ **snake** 名 ヘビ（蛇） 動（体を）くねらす，蛇行する

□ **snap** 動 ①ぱちっ［ぴしっ］という音を出す ②はじく，はじき飛ばす

□ **sneeze** 動 ①くしゃみをする ②鼻であしらう 名 くしゃみ

□ **snort** 動 鼻息を荒立てる，鼻を鳴らして不満などを表す，鼻で笑う 名 荒い鼻息

□ **snug-colored** 形 温かな色をした

□ **so** 熟 **and so** そこで，それだから **so ~ that** … 非常に～なので…

□ **so-called** 形 いわゆる，～といわれて

□ **sole** 形 唯一の，単独の 名 足の裏，靴底

□ **solitary** 形 ひとりの，孤独な，人里離れた

□ **some** 熟 **for some time** しばらくの間 **for some time now** これまでかなりの期間

□ **somehow** 副 ①どうにかこうにか，ともかく，何とかして ②どういうわけか

□ **someone** 代 ある人，誰か **take someone into**（人）を～の中に連れて行く

□ **someplace** 副 どこかで［へ・に］ 名 ある場所

□ **something** 代 ①ある物，何か ②いくぶん，多少

□ **sometime** 副 いつか，そのうち

□ **sometimes** 副 時々，時たま

□ **somewhat** 副 いくらか，やや，多少

□ **somewhere** 副 ①どこかへ［に］ ②いつか，およそ

□ **sown** 動 sow（まく）の過去分詞

□ **sparse** 形 まばらな，薄い，希薄な

□ **speak up** 率直に話す，はっきりしゃべる

□ **speaker** 名 話す人，演説者，代弁者

□ **speaking** 動 speak（話す）の現在分詞 形 話す，ものを言う 名 話すこと，談話，演説

□ **speechless** 形 無言の，口がきけない

□ **spiky** 形 先端のとがった，とげとげしい

□ **spin** 動 ぐるぐる回る，スピンする

□ **spineless** 形 意気地のない，ひ弱な，腰の抜けた

□ **spit** 動 吐く，つばを吐く 名 つば（を吐くこと）

□ **spite** 名 悪意，うらみ **in spite of** ～にもかかわらず

□ **spot** 名 ①地点，場所，立場 ②斑点，しみ 動 ①～を見つける ②点を打つ，しみをつける

□ **spurn** 動〔申し出・申し込みなどを〕はねつける，拒絶する

□ **squat** 動 しゃがむ 名 しゃがむこと

□ **stack** 名 ①大きな山，積み重ね ②多量，多数 動 積み重ねる

□ **stand out** 突き出る，目立つ

□ **starvation** 名 飢餓，餓死

☐ **starve** 動 ①餓死する，飢えさせる ②熱望する

☐ **state** 名 ①あり様，状態 ②国家，（アメリカなどの）州 ③階層，地位 動 述べる，表明する

☐ **statue** 名 像

☐ **steadily** 副 しっかりと

☐ **steam** 名 蒸気，湯気 動 湯気を立てる

☐ **steep** 形 険しい，法外な 動 漬ける，浸っている

☐ **step back** 後ずさりする，後に下がる

☐ **stick** 名 棒，枝 動 ①（突き）刺さる，刺す ②くっつく，くっつける ③突き出る ④《受け身形で》いきづまる **stick out** 突き出す

☐ **stiff** 形 ①堅い，頑固な ②堅苦しい

☐ **stifle** 動 ①窒息させる，息の根を止める ②鎮圧する

☐ **stimulate** 動 ①刺激する ②促す，活性化させる ③元気づける

☐ **stone** 名 ①石，小石 ②宝石 形 石の，石製の

☐ **stooped** 形 猫背の

☐ **stop doing** ～するのをやめる

☐ **straw** 名 麦わら，ストロー

☐ **straw-sandaled** 形 わら草履を履いた

☐ **stray** 動 ①はぐれる，道に迷う ②さまよう ③わきにそれる，本筋からはずれる

☐ **strength** 名 ①力，体力 ②長所，強み ③強度，濃度

☐ **stretch** 動 引き伸ばす，広がる，広げる **stretch out** 手足を伸ばす，広がる 名 伸ばす［伸びる］こと，広がり

☐ **stride** 動 ①大またで歩く ②またぐ 名 ①大またで歩くこと ②一またぎ

☐ **strip** 動 裸にする，脱衣する，はぐ，取り去る 名（細長い）1片

☐ **strode** 動 stride（大またで歩く）の過去

☐ **stroke** 名 ①一撃，一打ち ②一動作 ③一なで，一さすり 動 なでる，さする

☐ **struck** 動 strike（打つ）の過去，過去分詞

☐ **struggle** 動 もがく，奮闘する 名 もがき，奮闘

☐ **stubbornly** 副 頑固に，強情に

☐ **stuck** 動 stick（刺さる）の過去，過去分詞 **get stuck in** ～にはまり込む

☐ **stuffed** 形 詰まった，いっぱいになった，満腹して

☐ **stupendous** 形 驚くべき，大きな，並外れた

☐ **stutter** 動 口ごもりながら言う［話す］

☐ **style** 名 やり方，流儀，様式，スタイル

☐ **successively** 副 引き続いて

☐ **such a** そのような

☐ **such as** たとえば～，～のような

☐ **such ～ that ...** 非常に～なので…

☐ **sudden** 形 突然の，急な **all of a sudden** 突然，前触れもなしに

☐ **suffer** 動 ①（苦痛・損害などを）受ける，こうむる ②（病気に）なる，苦しむ，悩む

☐ **suikan** 名 水干《男性の平安装束のひとつ》

☐ **suit** 名 ①スーツ，背広 ②訴訟 ③ひとそろい，一組 動 ①適合する［させる］ ②似合う

☐ **sunlit** 形 太陽に照らされた

☐ **sunset** 名 日没，夕焼け

☐ **support** 動 ①支える，支持する ②養う，援助する 名 ①支え，支持 ②援助，扶養

☐ **surely** 副 確かに，きっと

☐ **surface** 名 ①表面，水面 ②うわべ，

外見 **on the surface of** ～の表面に

□ **surprising** 動 surprise（驚かす）の現在分詞 形 驚くべき，意外な

□ **surprisingly** 副 驚くほど（に），意外にも

□ **surrounding** 動 surround（囲む）の現在分詞 名《-s》周囲の状況，環境 形 周囲の

□ **survey** 動 ①見渡す ②概観する ③調査する 名 ①概観 ②調査

□ **survive** 動 ①生き残る，存続する，なんとかなる ②長生きする，切り抜ける

□ **sutra** 名《ヒンドゥー教・仏教》経典

□ **Suzaku Avenue** 朱雀大路《条坊制の都市において，宮城の正面から南方に向かって都を南北に走る道のこと》

□ **sway** 動 揺れる，揺れ動く，揺すぶる 名 揺れ，動揺

□ **sweat** 名 汗 動 汗をかく

□ **sweeping** 動 sweep（掃く）の現在分詞 形 一掃する，徹底的な 名 掃除，一掃

□ **sweetener** 名 甘味料

□ **sword** 名 ①剣，刀 ②武力

□ **swung** 動 swing（回転する）の過去，過去分詞

□ **symbol** 名 シンボル，象徴

□ **sympathy** 名 ①同情，思いやり，お悔やみ ②共鳴，同感

T

□ **tail** 名 ①尾，しっぽ ②後部，末尾 動 尾行する

□ **Takashima** 名 高島《地名》

□ **take advantage of** ～を利用する，～につけ込む

□ **take form** （物事が）形をとる，具体化する

□ **take from** ～から引く，選ぶ

□ **take place** 行われる，起こる

□ **take someone into** （人）を～の中に連れて行く

□ **take up** 取り上げる，やり始める

□ **take ～ to …** ～を…に連れて行く

□ **Tanba** 名 丹波《地名》

□ **tangerine** 名 タンジェリン《ミカンの一種》

□ **tap** 動 ①軽くポンとたたく，たたいて合図する ②栓を抜いて出す 名 ①軽くたたくこと ②蛇口，コック ③盗聴器

□ **task** 名（やるべき）仕事，職務，課題 動 仕事を課す，負担をかける

□ **taste** 名 ①味，風味 ②好み，趣味 動 味がする，味わう

□ **tasty** 形 おいしい

□ **tease** 動 いじめる，からかう，悩ます

□ **tell** 熟 **to tell the truth** 実は，実を言えば

□ **temple** 名 ①寺，神殿 ②こめかみ

□ **tend** 動 ①（～の）傾向がある，（～）しがちである ②面倒を見る，手入れをする

□ **than** 熟 **more than** ～以上 **more than enough** 十二分に，あり余るくらいに **rather than** ～よりむしろ

□ **that** 熟 **after that** その後 **now that** 今や～だから，～からには **so ～ that …** 非常に～なので… **such ～ that …** 非常に～なので… **this and that** あれやこれや **this way and that** あちこちへ

□ **thatch** 動〔家・屋根など〕を草［わら］でふく

□ **thatched** 形 わらぶき屋根の

□ **the more ～ the more …** ～すればするほどますます…

□ **the same ～ as [that] …** …と同じ（ような）～

□ **then** 熟 **even then** その時でさえ **now and then** ときどき **then and there** その場ですぐに

□ **there** 熟 **here and there** あちこちで **over there** あそこに **then and there** その場ですぐに **up there** あそこで

□ **these** 熟 **one of these days** いずれそのうちに，近日中に **one of these days** 近日中に，近いうちに **these days** このごろ

□ **thicket** 名 茂み，やぶ

□ **thickly** 副 厚く，深く，濃く

□ **thief** 名 泥棒，強盗

□ **thieves** 名 thief（泥棒）の複数

□ **thin** 形 薄い，細い，やせた，まばらな 副 薄く 動 薄く［細く］なる，薄くする

□ **think of** ～のことを考える，～を思いつく，考え出す

□ **thinking** 動 think（思う）の現在分詞 名 考えること，思考 形 思考力のある，考える

□ **thinly** 副 まばらに，細く，弱く，薄く

□ **this** 熟 **at this point** 現在のところ **at this time** 現時点では，このとき **in this way** このようにして **like this** このような，こんなふうに **this and that** あれやこれや **this one** これ，こちら **this way and that** あちこちへ

□ **those who** ～する人々

□ **though** 接 ①～にもかかわらず，～だが ②たとえ～でも **even though** ～であるけれども，～にもかかわらず 副 しかし

□ **throat** 名 のど，気管

□ **through** 熟 **go through** 通り抜ける **run through** 走り抜ける

□ **throughout** 前 ①～中，～を通じて ②～のいたるところに 副 初めから終わりまで，ずっと

□ **thrown** 動 throw（投げる）の過去分詞

□ **thrust** 動 ①強く押す，押しつける，突き刺す ②張り出す，突き出る 名 ①ぐいと押すこと，突き刺すこと ②《the –》要点

□ **thus** 副 ①このように ②これだけ ③かくて，だから

□ **tile** 名 タイル，瓦

□ **time** 熟 **at a time** 一度に，続けざまに **at the time** そのころ，当時は **at this time** 現時点では，このとき **for some time** しばらくの間 **for some time now** これまでかなりの期間 **for the first time** 初めて

□ **timidly** 副 こわごわ，臆病に

□ **timorous** 形 〔人や言動が〕臆病な，おずおずした

□ **tiny** 形 ちっぽけな，とても小さい

□ **tip** 名 先端，頂点

□ **tired** 動 tire（疲れる）の過去，過去分詞 形 ①疲れた，くたびれた ②あきた，うんざりした

□ **tirelessly** 副 疲れないで，たゆみなく

□ **to death** 死ぬまで，死ぬほど

□ **to one's feet** 両足で立っている状態に

□ **to tell the truth** 実は，実を言えば

□ **to the point of** 〔程度・段階などが〕～まで，～するまでに，～ほどに

□ **toad** 名 ヒキガエル

□ **toe** 名 足指，つま先

□ **token** 名 しるし，形見

□ **tone** 名 音，音色，調子 動 調和する［させる］

□ **tongue** 名 ①舌 ②弁舌 ③言語

□ **too much** 過度の

□ **topknot** 名 〔頭頂の〕頭髪，〔頭頂で束ねた〕髪形

□ **topmost** 形 最上位の，最上部の

□ **torch** 名 たいまつ，光明

□ **toss** 動投げる，放り上げる，上下に動く 名投げ上げ，トス

□ **tranquil** 形静かな，穏やかな

□ **transform** 動 ①変形［変化］する，変える ②変換する

□ **transmit** 動 ①送る ②伝える，伝わる ③感染させる

□ **trap** 名わな，策略 動わなを仕掛ける，わなで捕らえる

□ **traveler** 名旅行者

□ **treat** 動 ①扱う ②治療する ③おごる 名 ①おごり，もてなし，ごちそう ②楽しみ

□ **treetop** 名こずえ，木のてっぺん

□ **trembling** 形〔物・身体の一部・声などが〕震える

□ **trick** 名 ①策略 ②いたずら，冗談 ③手品，錯覚 動だます

□ **tried** 動 try（試みる）の過去，過去分詞 形試験済みの，信頼できる

□ **trivial** 形 ①ささいな ②平凡な

□ **trousers** 名ズボン

□ **truly** 副 ①全く，本当に，真に ②心から，誠実に

□ **truth** 名 ①真理，事実，本当 ②誠実，忠実さ **to tell the truth** 実は，実を言えば

□ **trying** 動 try（やってみる）の現在分詞 形つらい，苦しい，しゃくにさわる

□ **Tsuruga** 名敦賀《地名》

□ **tub** 名桶，浴槽

□ **tuck** 動 ①押し込む，隠す ②はさみ込む 名 ①縫いひだ，タック ②押し込むこと

□ **tumble** 動倒れる，転ぶ，つまずく 名転倒，混乱状態

□ **turn around** 振り向く，向きを変える

□ **turn away** 向こうへ行く，それる，（顔を）そむける

□ **turn into** ～に変わる

□ **turn on** ～の方を向く

□ **turn out** ～と判明する，（結局～に）なる

□ **turn to** ～の方を向く

□ **twilight** 名夕暮れ，薄明かり

□ **twisted** 動 twist（ねじる）の過去・過去分詞 形ねじれた

□ **twister** 名竜巻，辻風

U

□ **Uji** 名宇治《地名》

□ **unable** 形《be – to ～》～することができない

□ **unbelievably** 副信じられないほど

□ **unchanged** 形変化していない

□ **unconsciously** 副無意識に，知らず知らずに

□ **undaunted** 形くじけない，ひるまない

□ **underfoot** 副足元に

□ **undergarment** 名下着，肌着

□ **understanding** 動 understand（理解する）の現在分詞 名理解，意見の一致，了解 形理解のある，思いやりのある

□ **undistinguished** 形平凡な，他と異なる特徴のない，目立たない

□ **undisturbed** 形邪魔されない，乱されない，平穏な

□ **undoubtedly** 副疑う余地なく

□ **unease** 名不安，心配，困惑

□ **uneasiness** 名不安，心配

□ **uneasy** 形不安な，焦って

□ **unexpected** 形思いがけない，予期しない

□ **unforgivable** 形〔過ちなどが〕許せない，容赦できない，弁解［言い訳］できない

□ **unfortunately** 副不幸にも，運悪く

□ **unimpressive** 形印象的でない

□ **uninviting** 形〔場所などが〕興味をそそらない，魅力的でない

□ **university** 名（総合）大学

□ **unknown** 形知られていない，不明の

□ **unlike** 形似ていない，違った 前～と違って

□ **unmovably** 副動かない，不動に

□ **unofficial** 形〔行為が〕非公式［公認］の

□ **unpainted** 形〔部屋・家具などが〕塗料を塗っていない，未塗装の

□ **unpolished** 形〔磨かれていなくて〕滑らかでない，輝いていない

□ **unsheathed** 形被鞘のない

□ **unsteady** 形不安定な，不規則な

□ **unsure** 形確かでない，自信がない

□ **unusual** 形普通でない，珍しい，見［聞き］慣れない

□ **unwillingly** 副不本意に，いやいや

□ **up there** あそこで

□ **up to** ～まで，～に至るまで，～に匹敵して，《be –》～しようとしている

□ **upon** 前①《場所・接触》～（の上）に ②《日・時》～に ③《関係・従事》～に関して，～について，～して 副前へ，続けて

□ **upside** 名上側，上部

□ **urge** 動①せき立てる，強力に推し進める，かりたてる ②《- … to ～》…に～するよう熱心に勧める 名衝動，かりたてられるような気持ち

□ **urine** 名尿，小便

□ **use** 熟 **make use of** ～を利用する，～を生かす

□ **used** 動①use（使う）の過去，過去分詞 ②《– to》よく～したものだ，以前は～であった 形①慣れている，《get [become] – to》～に慣れてくる ②使われた，中古の

□ **useless** 形役に立たない，無益な

□ **utter** 形完全な，まったくの 動（声・言葉を）発する

V

□ **vacantly** 副〔人の心・表情などが〕ぼんやりと，ぽかんと

□ **valet** 名〔身の回りの世話をする男性の〕近侍，従者

□ **vanish** 動姿を消す，消える，ゼロになる

□ **various** 形変化に富んだ，さまざまの，たくさんの

□ **vassal** 名〔封建時代の〕臣下

□ **velvet** 名ベルベット，ビロード状のもの

□ **verge** 名①へり，縁，端 ②境界 ③瀬戸際

□ **vex** 動うるさがらせる，悩ませる

□ **victim** 名犠牲者，被害者

□ **violent** 形暴力的な，激しい

□ **virtually** 副事実上，ほぼ，～も同然で

W

□ **wad** 動〔～を〕丸める，詰め物をする［いっぱいにする］

□ **wagtail** 名《鳥》セキレイ

□ **wait for** ～を待つ

□ **waiting** 動wait（待つ）の現在分詞 名待機，給仕すること 形待っている，仕えている

□ **walk along** （前へ）歩く，～に沿って歩く

□ **walking** 動walk（歩く）の現在分詞 名歩行，歩くこと 形徒歩の，歩行用の

- □ **wander** 動 ①さまよう，放浪する，横道へそれる ②放心する
- □ **ward** 名 行政区
- □ **warmth** 名 暖かさ，思いやり
- □ **washed-out** 形 洗いざらしの，色あせた，くたびれた
- □ **wave** 名 ①波 ②(手などを)振ること 動 ①揺れる，揺らす，波立つ ②(手などを振って)合図する
- □ **waver** 動 心が揺らぐ，揺れ動く，ぐらつく
- □ **wax tree** 《植物》ハゼノキ
- □ **way** 熟 **all the way** ずっと，はるばる **go out of one's way to** わざわざ〜する，〜するために尽力する **in no way** 決して〜でない **in this way** このようにして **lead the way** 先に立って導く，案内する，率先する **make one's way to** 〜に向かって進む **on one's way** 出て行く，出掛ける **this way and that** あちこちへ **way of** 〜する方法
- □ **weak-kneed** 形 弱腰の，優柔不断の
- □ **wearily** 副 疲れて
- □ **weight** 名 ①重さ，重力，体重 ②重荷，負担 ③重大さ，勢力 動 ①重みをつける ②重荷を負わせる
- □ **well** 熟 **as well as** 〜と同様に
- □ **well-wadded** 形 〔綿が〕よく詰まった
- □ **westering** 形 西に向かう［進む・傾く］
- □ **what** 熟 **no matter what** たとえどんな〜であろうと
- □ **whatever** 代 ①《関係代名詞》〜するものは何でも ②どんなこと［もの］が〜とも 形 ①どんな〜でも ②《否定文・疑問文で》少しの〜も，何らかの
- □ **whenever** 接 ①〜するときはいつでも，〜するたびに ②いつ〜しても
- □ **whet** 動 ①(刃物を)とぐ ②(食欲・興味を)そそる
- □ **whether** 接 〜かどうか，〜かまたは…，〜であろうとなかろうと
- □ **while** 熟 **for a while** しばらくの間，少しの間
- □ **whimpering** 名 〔人が〕めそめそと泣くこと
- □ **whip** 動 ①むちうつ ②急に動く［動かす］ 名 むち
- □ **white-haired** 形 白髪の
- □ **whitebait** 名 《魚》シラス
- □ **who** 熟 **those who** 〜する人々
- □ **whole** 形 全体の，すべての，完全な，満〜，丸〜 名 《the –》全体，全部
- □ **whom** 代 ①誰を［に］ ②《関係代名詞》〜するところの人，そしてその人を
- □ **wicked** 形 悪い，不道徳な
- □ **wide** 形 幅の広い，広範囲の，幅が〜ある 副 広く，大きく開いて
- □ **wide-eyed** 形 〔驚嘆・疑い・感動などで〕目を大きく見開いた
- □ **widespread** 形 広範囲におよぶ，広く知られた
- □ **wield** 動 ①(道具などを)巧みに使う ②(権力などを)振るう
- □ **wig** 名 かつら
- □ **wildly** 副 荒々しく，乱暴に，むやみに
- □ **willing** 形 ①喜んで〜する，〜しても構わない，いとわない ②自分から進んで行う
- □ **willow** 名 ヤナギ(柳)
- □ **wipe** 動 〜をふく，ぬぐう，ふきとる 名 ふくこと
- □ **wish for** 所望する
- □ **with all** 〜がありながら
- □ **within** 前 ①〜の中［内］に，〜の内部に ②〜以内で，〜を越えないで 副 中［内］へ［に］，内部に 名 内部
- □ **witness** 名 ①証拠，証言 ②目撃者 動 ①目撃する ②証言する

☐ **witticism** 名機知に富む言葉，しゃれ

☐ **witty** 形機知に富んだ，気のきいた

☐ **woke** 動 wake（目が覚める）の過去

☐ **wonder** 動 ①不思議に思う，（～に）驚く ②（～かしらと）思う **wonder if** ～ではないかと思う 名驚き（の念），不思議なもの

☐ **wooden** 形木製の，木でできた

☐ **wooden-hilted** 形 木の柄の

☐ **wordlessly** 副黙ったまま

☐ **working** 動 work（働く）の現在分詞 形働く，作業の，実用的な

☐ **world** 熟 **everything in the world** この世にある全ての物

☐ **worry about** ～のことを心配する

☐ **worth** 形（～の）価値がある，（～）しがいがある 名価値，値打ち

☐ **worthy** 形価値のある，立派な

☐ **would like to** ～したいと思う

☐ **wretched** 形哀れな，困った，みじめな，ひどい

☐ **wrinkle** 名しわ 動しわが寄る，しわを寄せる

☐ **writer** 名書き手，作家

Y

☐ **yam** 名ヤム（イモ）

☐ **Yamashina** 名山科《地名》

☐ **yawn** 名あくび 動あくびをする

☐ **years** 熟 **for ～ years** ～年間，～年にわたって

☐ **yellowish** 形黄色っぽい，黄色がかった

☐ **yellowish-white** 形黄色がかった白色の，黄白色の

☐ **yet** 熟 **not yet** まだ～してない

ラダーシリーズ

Rashomon / Yam Gruel

羅生門・芋粥――芥川龍之介傑作選

2021年5月8日　第1刷発行

原著者　芥川龍之介

リライト　マイケル・ブレーズ

発行者　浦　晋亮

発行所　IBCパブリッシング株式会社
〒162-0804 東京都新宿区中里町29番3号
菱秀神楽坂ビル9F
Tel. 03-3513-4511　Fax. 03-3513-4512
www.ibcpub.co.jp

印　刷　株式会社シナノパブリッシングプレス
装　丁　伊藤 理恵
イラスト　ミヤザーナツ

Printed in Japan
ISBN978-4-7946-0657-0